Beginner's Guide to Growing Baby

Beginner's Guide to Growing Baby:

Tips to Help You Through all Four Trimesters

Bonnie Way and Anna Eastland

We are not medical experts; we are simply sharing what we've learned from our own research and experience. We encourage you to discuss any pregnancy concerns with your doctor or midwife.

To Sunshine, Lily, Jade, Pearl and Joey,

who made me a mom and

have given me my biggest adventure.

I love you forever.

~ B.W.

To all my fellow moms,

especially my dear mom buddies,

who help turn the challenges of motherhood

into an awesome adventure.

We're all in this together!

May your babies bring you lots of joy!

~ A. E.

Table of Contents

Labour & Birth

Fourth Trimester

Birth Stories

Why Birth Education Is Necessary

During my second pregnancy, I read a blog post about birth conversations. The blogger wished she had become more educated about the birth process before having her first son. Her reflections on the fact that we talk about birth *after* it has happened, more than before, made me think about my own birthing experiences.

When I was three months pregnant with Sunshine, my husband and I dropped by my best friend's place. Her three older sisters were there too, with their kids, and my hubby waited until all the women were within hearing distance to announce our news. As they descended on me with congratulations, he slipped away.

Then one of the sisters asked, "Have you heard about the local midwife program?" She raved about her experience there, mentioning water birth and a 40-minute labour.

At the time, I was seeing a doctor for my prenatal care, but I wasn't happy with him. My appointments were generally ten minutes—a quick check of blood pressure, urine, and weight and then he was on to the next patient.

That was my first pregnancy, so I didn't know what to expect or what to ask. I felt like he had no time for me and wasn't providing me with any information. At one visit, he gave me a sheaf of papers with instructions to drop by the lab and take the tests, but never explained what any of the tests were. So I went to an info session with the midwives and switched my care.

After an initial half-hour consultation with the midwife—in which she went over those tests the doctor had ordered and explained what all of them were—I began group appointments. I and about seven other women met with one of the three midwives for an hour and a half. Each of us checked our own weight, urine, and blood pressure and recorded it in our charts.

I loved feeling like I knew what was going on with my body and my baby. The midwife checked our charts and our bellies. Then they had a discussion topic for us, ranging from pregnancy nutrition to what to expect during labour. They kept us informed about what to expect at the hospital, from them, and during our pregnancy. The other women—some of whom were having their second or third baby—often asked questions I hadn't thought of myself but wanted to know.

When I was five months pregnant, we visited friends of ours who had had their baby just after our wedding. Their desire for a natural birth had taken them to a birthing centre in the United States because the midwives in Ontario wouldn't provide the care they wanted. Their commitment to having that natural birth carried them through forty hours of labour, with no interventions and no drugs. They honestly shared all of this with us, without pressure or judgments, and I soaked in what they told us and thought about it for months.

> I was grateful to the women who took time to share their pregnancy experiences and birth stories with me and to point me towards resources that had influenced and helped them.

She introduced me to Henci Goer's book *The Thinking Woman's Guide to a Better Birth* and Robert Bradley's book *Husband-Coached Childbirth: The Bradley Method of Natural Childbirth*. I read the second book aloud to my husband while we drove back and forth to visit our parents on the weekends. Both books profoundly impacted my views on pregnancy and birth and what I wanted as my pregnancy progressed.

Despite all these preparations, I still wondered what labour would be like. I knew it was different for every woman, even for every baby. Yet I was grateful to the women who took time to share their pregnancy experiences and birth stories with me and to point me towards resources that had influenced and helped them.

2

I had a fairly textbook, ten-hour labour with Sunshine. And I thought the second time around would be easier because I'd know what to expect—I'd already done it once.

Instead, Lily's birth was a new learning process. We had moved since Sunshine's birth and Alberta had given full funding to midwives. As a result, the midwives were completely booked and I couldn't get one.

However, the doctors in our small town were just as busy. I liked the doctor who did my prenatal care—she was great with Sunshine (who attended all of my appointments), agreed to my request not to have an ultrasound, and didn't worry too much about the fact that I wasn't gaining as much weight as she expected.

However, she couldn't deliver the baby, so I had to switch to another doctor—a new, young doctor whose attitude was "I am the doctor and you are the patient so you'll do what I say."

As I stressed over what the doctor ordered and what I wanted at Lily's birth, I turned to research. I spent hours online and borrowed stacks of books from the library. I talked to friends of mine who had similar birthing ideas to mine.

In the end, Lily's birth went better than I feared—even though I sometimes wonder if my stress over her birth caused her to be born a week late and caused my labour to go slower.

As I approached the birth of my third child—with a midwife in British Columbia, after another move—I thought about all those issues again. My midwives presented everything about birth as an option; I had the option of receiving pain medication in labour or not; I had the option of giving my baby the vitamin K shot after birth or not.

The midwives explained the pros and cons but left the decision up to me—the mom. And that's the attitude I carried with me for my next pregnancies and births. I enjoyed talking with my midwife about my prenatal care and what might happen during labour and what my options were—what the best option was for *me* and for *this* baby.

We as women need to educate ourselves about birth and everything that goes with it. Even if we have a great doctor or a great midwife, we need to know what our options are so we can make the best choices—choices that might be different for each woman and even for each pregnancy.

Browse websites, read books (like this one!), talk to friends. Even negative birthing stories can be helpful if you don't let them scare you but propel you into some research—as I recently did when a new acquaintance mentioned a birth complication I'd never heard about before. Information is powerful.

We as women do need to educate ourselves about birth and everything that goes with it.

If you're not sure where to start in your birth education, I've included a list of my favourite birthing books at the end of this book. I've also written out my full birthing stories in the hopes that they will inspire and reassure you with the way a normal, natural birth goes.

First Trimester

The first time I thought it was the stomach flu,
and refused to eat,
but then it was miraculously cured
by ginger ale and pizza…
No ordinary flu!

A few minutes in the bathroom reveal
two thin, blue lines pointing to a new direction,
running parallel towards the horizon
with common purpose.
Two lives connected more intimately than before,
the empty space between them
no longer empty.

There's new life nestled within,
so tiny I can't yet hear the heartbeat,
though the book says it starts at 26 days.

I'm flooded with the hope-filled mystery
of holding a child within me,
yet nervous because I can
barely hold in my lunch.

How can I be strong enough
to protect this life,
when I can't stop falling asleep on the couch?

How can I be a mother,
when I feel so fragile
that all I want is to curl up into a ball
and be tucked into bed?

Welcome to the wisdom of women,
who have the courage it takes
to be vulnerable,
the strength it takes
to suffer for love,
and the power to let go of control
and let something bigger take place,
this mystery of life,
blooming like a flower in the dark.

~ Anna Eastland

CHAPTER ONE

How to Choose the Right Care Provider

One of the first things you need to do when becoming pregnant (or even when thinking about trying to conceive) is find a prenatal care provider. This could be a midwife, family doctor, or ob-gyn (depending on your medical history and needs).

After having five babies and living in seven different cities, I've experienced my share of doctors and prenatal care and the stress of finding the right care giver during pregnancy.

Depending on where you live, there may be limited care providers able to help you, so you need to get on their list as soon as you can.

Call doctors and midwives and ask if they are taking new clients, what their intake procedure is, if they have a waiting list, when you can meet them, etc.

When I realized I was pregnant with Lily, Alberta faced a shortage of both midwives and doctors. It was hard to get a family doctor and even harder to get a midwife. I ended up having to switch prenatal care providers towards the end of my pregnancy. I also ended up with a doctor whom I didn't like, but I didn't have any other options for care providers.

I like asking my friends for recommendations to prenatal care providers. I found out about my first midwife through my best friend's older sister. My third midwife (with my fourth daughter) was also recommended to me by a friend. I found my last midwife by doing a Google search for a midwife in our area of the city.

You want a care provider you trust and are comfortable with. Labour is the worst pain you will likely (hopefully!) have to endure in your life. When you're in labour, you want to be focused on the baby and what your body is telling you to do and not on how you dislike your care provider. If something about the doctor's manner bothers you during your initial or prenatal visits, I would recommend trying to find another doctor.

One thing I like about the midwifery model of care is that the midwives take time to get to know you. A midwife practice is generally smaller than a doctor's; my midwives have worked in teams of either two or three. My appointments rotate between each of the midwives, so I've seen them all several times by the time I go into labour. That way I'm well acquainted with whomever will show up when I call to say I'm in labour.

During my second pregnancy, I had several prenatal appointments with the doctor who was supposed to attend my birth. However, whether or not she could be there depended on when I went into labour. Doctors do need to sleep, after all! And then she went away for a weekend, and I ended up with the doctor on call—a man I'd never met before (and never saw again).

Your care provider should take the time to listen to your questions and concerns and respond to them. In my first two pregnancies, I had two doctors who were either too busy to explain my choices to me or didn't feel they needed to do this. As an independent woman with (now) two degrees, I really disliked being treated that way. Your care provider should clearly explain any tests or procedures they expect you to complete (and why they recommend these) and respect you as a woman.

There are a lot of choices you'll have to make during your pregnancy. If this is your first pregnancy, the choices can be overwhelming. You can consult your care provider, husband, friends and books like this, but the choice is still up to you. Your care provider and friends should respect that.

I recommend writing down questions to ask at your appointments. I've often forgotten something I wanted to talk about until after my appointment. Try to ask the big questions at your first appointment to get an idea about the style of care offered and whether that agrees with the care you want.

A pregnancy journal can be a great way to keep track of your questions, ideas, concerns, doctor's recommendations, learning, etc.

Finally, an important part of choosing your care provider is where you'll deliver the baby. I really dislike the drive to the hospital when I'm in labour (which is one reason I chose to have homebirths for my last three babies). If possible, choose the hospital that's closest to you or easiest to get to. (Think about rush hour—you don't know when you'll go into labour and you don't want to get stuck in traffic!)

Make sure to ask your doctor or midwife where he or she has hospital privileges. I had to switch doctors halfway through Lily's prenatal care because my family doctor couldn't attend births at the hospital. Continuity of care is important, so try to determine early where you'll be delivering and which doctor can be there.

While I've had each of my five babies in a different place with a different birthing team, many of my friends have had the same team help them deliver their babies in the same place. Anna's midwives have been with her for all eight of her births. Hopefully, the relationships you develop with your doctor or midwife in your first pregnancy will continue into your next pregnancies.

CHAPTER TWO

Telling Older Siblings about a New Baby

One of the things that was fun with my third, fourth and fifth pregnancies was how excited my older daughters were about the baby. They have always been overjoyed about and impatient to meet their new little sibling. Here are my tips for telling older siblings about a new baby.

1. Don't tell your children before you are ready to tell your family and friends.

When I was about one month pregnant with our third baby, my husband told the girls, "There's a baby in Mommy's tummy."

I looked at him in surprise because we'd agreed to wait a few months before telling our family and friends about the baby. I didn't think the girls would be able to keep the secret, but surprisingly, we only talked about it at home.

Until my aunt visited. Then Sunshine told her twice, "There's a baby in Mommy's tummy!" The first time she said it, we were leaving the house and my aunt didn't seem to hear. The second time, my aunt looked at me for confirmation. It ended up being a very cute way to share the news.

My advice would be to tell your children before telling others. They should hear it from you instead of a friend or relative, but don't expect them to keep the secret for very long.

2. Look at baby pictures together.

Often when we talk about the baby, I pull out the girls' baby photo albums. We look at the pictures of them as tiny babies, including pictures of Sunshine holding Lily when she was born. The girls love seeing themselves as babies along with pictures of various family members who came to visit after they were born.

You can find various books at your library or bookstore about new babies. *The New Baby* by Mercer Mayer (Little Critter series), *The Berenstain Bear's New Baby* by Stan and Jan Berenstain and *Ninja Baby* by David Zeltser all talk about big siblings adjusting to a new baby's arrival in a positive manner.

Everywhere Babies by Susan Meyers is a cute board book about baby's first year. *101 Things to Do with Baby* by Jan Ormerod has helpful tips for older siblings who want to be involved with the baby. These are both great ways to prepare toddlers or preschoolers for what it will be like to have a new baby around.

Hello in There: A Big Sister's Book of Waiting by Jo Witek is an adorable lift-the-flap book about pregnancy and an impatient big sister. This was Pearl's favourite book when she was waiting for Joey to be born. They are my babies closest in age, and it was cute to see Pearl connecting with the story as she waited for her baby brother to come.

3. Meet your child where she is.

Something coming in the future is a tough concept for toddlers to grasp. Even explaining to a two-year-old that an event is going to happen next weekend leaves them a bit confused. For a while, I stopped telling my daughters about exciting events coming up (like a grandparents' visit) because they'd ask me every single day until it happened if TODAY was the day.

When telling your children about a new baby, try to meet them where they are. Children under age two may not understand something they can't see, like a baby hiding in Mommy's tummy.

When I was expecting Lily, we tried many times to explain to Sunshine that there was a baby coming. My husband would hide dolls under his shirt and compare that bump to my baby bump, then pull the doll out. It didn't work. Once Lily was born, however, Sunshine was all over her baby sister.

There's a larger gap between my second and third daughters, so Lily was older than Sunshine was when we told her about Jade's upcoming arrival. Lily at age three seemed better able to grasp the idea of a baby in my tummy. Either that or she was simply picking up on Sunshine's excitement!

When we announced my fifth pregnancy to our older daughters, I saw different wheels turning in my nine-year-old's head. As a tween, she now had other questions about babies and where they come from. She also knew about fussy babies and limited space. She still viewed the baby with excitement. Our conversations with her about baby's arrival were different than with our two-year-old.

4. Talk about the baby.

Children under age two may not understand something they can't see, like a baby hiding in Mommy's tummy.

We talked about the baby lots, even before we spread the news to our friends and extended family. We asked the girls what we should name the baby. (When Sunshine was two, she suggested names like Mike the Knight or Dora.) Lily said she'd share her Pooh Bear blanket with the baby. They all liked kissing the baby (aka my tummy). They even suggested things to get for the baby when we were out shopping.

For nearly all of my prenatal appointments, I've had all the older children come along. With Joey, that meant I had all four girls crowded into the midwife's office, eager to "help" with the Doppler or measuring tape. Once we got home, the girls often asked if they could "check the baby." I'd lie on the couch so they could feel my tummy as they'd seen the midwife do.

The girls were also excited to help sort baby clothes, set up the crib, and do other tasks related to the new baby's arrival.

We tried to honestly answer all their questions about the baby. Even when I was struggling with excitement over my fifth pregnancy, I kept it positive for them. We involved them in problem solving for where the baby should sleep and talked about how they could help once baby arrived.

5. Give older siblings a gift to celebrate baby's arrival.

At Lily's baptism, one of my friends brought a present for Sunshine so she wouldn't feel left out by all the presents Lily was getting. That stuffed lamb became Sunshine's favourite toy for years to come.

For Jade's arrival, I bought Sunshine and Lily new shirts to help share the news about the baby. In sparkly letters, Sunshine's shirt said "I'm Going to Be a Big Sister Again" and Lily's said "I'm Going to Be a Big Sister." They were super excited about the new shirts—and about telling everyone they really *were* going to be big sisters.

Friends of ours passed on two huge bins of MegaBloks, which helped keep the girls busy while I was taking care of the baby. And my aunt got them new books, which I could read to them while I was nursing Jade.

We've never encountered sibling jealousy or anxiety over a new baby's arrival. I hope with these tips, your children will also be delighted to welcome their newest family member home.

CHAPTER THREE

Dealing with Morning Sickness

Morning sickness. That dreaded companion to most pregnancies.

I've always been surprised that, when baby is so tiny, my body reacts so strongly to his or her presence. For most women, morning sickness occurs only during the first trimester, but it may last right up until baby's birth.

The name is also misleading, as few women have it only in the morning (although you may feel the worst immediately after waking).

My morning sickness has gradually worsened with each of my pregnancies. It has started a bit earlier and lasted a bit longer. Other women have found that they have worse morning sickness if their baby is a certain gender. If your mom had easy pregnancies, you might also have little morning sickness—but I also know sisters who have had very different reactions to pregnancy.

Managing your morning sickness will likely be a pregnancy-by-pregnancy, month-by-month, day-by-day affair. Here are some tips that have helped me (and friends of mine).

1. Wake up slowly.

If you tend to get out of bed and head straight for the toilet, try to get up more slowly. Put a glass of water and a granola bar or muffin beside your bed at night. In the morning, sip your water and nibble your snack before you sit up. Alternatively, you could see if your husband is willing to get you breakfast in bed during this time.

Having some food in your stomach may help prevent the nausea. Your body may also prefer different foods; try dry toast (easy on the stomach) or a fried egg (protein) to see which works better.

2. Snack regularly.

During my first pregnancy, I was able to manage my morning sickness by keeping a stash of granola bars in my desk drawer and purse. I had breakfast, mid-morning snack, lunch, afternoon snack, supper, and bedtime snack. Sometimes I had more snacks.

I felt as if I was eating like a horse! However, on most days, as long as I had some protein in my stomach, I felt less nauseous. Having small meals or snacks more frequently, rather than three big meals a day as we usually do, can help your stomach.

3. Try ginger and peppermint.

Ginger can help stave off nausea. A friend gave me some Chinese ginger candies during one pregnancy (and I still have a few kicking around my purse and cupboards!). Sucking or chewing on these candies throughout the day helped me spend less time bent over the toilet.

If you like tea, try ginger tea or peppermint tea. Teas can help you stay hydrated as well as less nauseous.

4. Avoid strong smells and certain foods.

I worked at a coffee shop as a barista during my second pregnancy. Customers and friends were often surprised that the smell of coffee didn't trigger my nausea. I wasn't able to work the opening shifts, but I loved the smell of coffee.

Strong smells can often trigger unexpected reactions during pregnancy. One of my friends can't stand the smell of red meat when she's expecting. Her poor husband has to eat out if he's craving steak. Another friend of mine gave me a pound of coffee beans she'd just opened, as they made her want to puke. Listen to your body at these times and avoid the smells or foods that trigger a strong reaction.

Foods that you previously loved now may make you dash for the washroom. Usually, this will pass with your morning sickness or baby's arrival. Pregnancy cravings and aversions aren't totally understood, but your body is trying to tell you something, so go with it.

5. Talk to your prenatal care provider.

I was able to manage my morning sickness with food during my first pregnancy, but I asked my care providers for a prescription for my last four pregnancies. I always try natural remedies first, but I also need to be able to function on a certain level, and medication helps.

Morning sickness medication didn't make me feel 100 percent again, but it did take the edge off my nausea and exhaustion. That helped me get to work during my second pregnancy, and chase my older kids during my third, fourth and fifth pregnancies.

Talk to your prenatal care provider about your morning sickness. Some women are so affected by extreme morning sickness that medication is necessary for their health and the baby's. Be honest with your care provider about your weight loss or gain, how much food you are able to keep down, and how often you are throwing up.

CHAPTER FOUR

Cold Remedies for Pregnant Moms

The first hints of a sore throat always leave me thinking, "No, not again!" I might add a few stronger words to that phrase as I think about the runny nose and cough that soon follow and the fact I can do very little to deal with those. Colds are annoying enough to a normal person. When I'm pregnant and can't resort to over-the-counter medications to help ease symptoms, well, a cold is more than just annoying.

Because I've been either pregnant or breastfeeding for the better part of the last dozen years, I've spent a lot of time looking for ways to fight colds without turning to drugs. Here's what I've learned about treating cold symptoms.

One of the best and simplest remedies for a cold is rest. My dad swore by this remedy. Pregnancy can be tiring on its own, and this added exhaustion may hinder the body's ability to fight a cold. Heidi Murkoff and her co-authors in *What to Expect When You're Expecting* say, "Taking a cold to bed doesn't necessarily shorten its duration, but if your body is begging for some rest, be sure to listen."

While sleeping or lying down, use extra pillows or a body pillow to elevate your head; this may ease a stuffy nose and prevent coughing.

Increasing your fluids is also important for fighting off a virus. Murkoff explains, "Fever, sneezes and a runny nose will cause your body to lose fluids that you and your body need." Try drinking hot teas (such as lemon or ginger), chicken soup, and hot, diluted grapefruit or orange juice. Or keep a cup of water close and sip regularly.

To treat a sore throat, make a cup of tea with lots of honey. I like to add a teaspoon of honey and a teaspoon of lemon juice to a cup of boiling water. Gargling warm salt water may also help your throat feel better while getting rid of any bacteria too.

Cough drops such as Halls or Vicks Vitamin C Drops can also soothe a sore throat. Boiron Roxalia is a homeopathic sore throat remedy that is safe to take during pregnancy.

Vicks VapoRub, or similar products (such as natural DIY recipes you can find on Pinterest), help with congestion and coughing. Simply rub this on your chest or under your nose to clear sinuses. Rubbing Vicks on your nose also helps prevent your nose from turning red and irritated from frequent Kleenex use.

A hot shower or a humidifier may also help. In *It Worked For Me: 1001 Real-Life Pregnancy Tips*, Michelle Kennedy recommends using "eucalyptus, lavender, lemon and tea tree . . . for congestion: put two drops of each essential oil into a bowl of hot water, then place a towel over your head and inhale the steam for 10 minutes."

Dr. William Sears suggests flushing nasal passages with saltwater nose drops. My brother swears by his neti pot when he has a cold. I have found it difficult to use and prefer homeopathic remedies like A. Vogel's Sinna, a sinus spray that can help with acute and chronic congestion.

Herbal remedies can also be effective in treating colds. Kennedy recommends a tea made from four whole dried cloves, one tsp coriander seeds, a few slices of fresh ginger, one pint water, a slice of honey, and lemon. Boil the herbs and water together for twenty minutes, then add the lemon and boil for another five minutes before straining and sweetening the tea with honey. She says "cloves have antiseptic and stimulant qualities, coriander seeds aid digestion, honey is soothing to the throat, and ginger is soothing to the stomach."

A. Vogel's Echinaforce tincture can be used when pregnant and breastfeeding. It is clinically shown to help prevent and relive the symptoms of colds and flus and to support the immune system. Take it at the first signs of infection, with water. I've found it to be quite effective in preventing or reducing cold symptoms.

Garlic also boosts the immune system. Add more garlic while cooking meals, though garlic is best (and worst!) taken raw. Mix crushed or finely chopped garlic with butter or margarine and spread it on a slice of toast for a quick snack. Or mince a clove of garlic, add some olive oil and parmesan cheese, and serve it on salad or use it as a dip for bread. I also make hummus using a few extra cloves of garlic.

If you find yourself turning to comfort foods like chicken noodle soup when sick, that's great! Try to avoid packaged chicken noodle soup as it is likely high in salt and low in helpfulness. Make homemade soup with chicken broth, noodles or rice, and a few teaspoons of lemon juice.

You could also grab a whole roast chicken at the grocery store. (Who wants to cook while pregnant *and* sick anyway?) After you've finished the chicken, boil the bones and some vegetables for several hours (or pop them into your Instant Pot to save time) and strain off the broth to make your own soup.

Taking extra vitamins is another way to give your immune system a boost at this time. Kennedy notes that "any food rich in Vitamin C may help prevent colds… and ease [symptoms] once you've got them." Try citrus fruits (oranges, grapefruit), broccoli, tomatoes, cabbage, blackberries or raspberries, mango or papaya, or cantaloupe.

If you find yourself turning to comfort foods like chicken noodle soup when sick, that's great!

Vitamin C supplements are available, but large doses of vitamin C should be avoided when pregnant. Too much can cause diarrhea.

Another important vitamin during pregnancy is zinc. Zinc helps with your baby's development, healing wounds and boosting your immune system. Like Vitamin C, it's available as a supplement, but too much of it can cause nausea or diarrhea (especially if your prenatal vitamins already contain zinc). Try to eat zinc-rich foods such as red meat, beans, nuts, and dairy products.

Avoiding sugar is probably one of the hardest "remedies" for me to follow, but sugar weakens your body's immune system. On his website, Dr. Sears explains, "Eating or drinking 100 grams (8 tbsp.) of sugar, the equivalent of about two cans of soda, can reduce the ability of white blood cells to kill germs by forty percent. The immune-suppressing effect of sugar starts less than thirty minutes after ingestion and may last for five hours."

Reducing your sugar intake when you feel cold symptoms starting will help your immune system fight off the cold.

Finally, a cold may simply be a good reminder to take a break and take care of yourself. Sometimes all you can do is go to bed and wait for the virus to run its course. Ask for help if you can, turn on the TV for your toddler if necessary, and surround yourself with tea and tissues.

CHAPTER FIVE

Exercising for a Healthy Pregnancy

If you're dealing with morning sickness and first trimester exhaustion, exercise is likely the last thing on your mind. Many of us know we have to cut back on some things we enjoy (like drinking and skiing!) during pregnancy and may unconsciously add exercise to that list. But exercise during pregnancy can help reduce discomfort and increase your strength for labour.

The International Food Information Council Foundation recommends pregnant women do thirty minutes of moderate physical activity daily (or nearly every day).

Dr. Robert Bradley compares birth to a marathon. In *Husband-Coached Childbirth,* he asks, "If you knew you were going to run a marathon in nine months, wouldn't you train?" Think of prenatal exercise as training for labour.

Prenatal exercise may get more difficult as your growing tummy gets in the way, but you can adjust your workout or type of exercise to accommodate baby. Your prenatal care provider may have pamphlets for local classes catering to pregnant women, such as prenatal aquafit. These are sometimes offered through local community centres, baby stores, or gyms.

Pick exercises that are easy on your body and your baby. Walking is gentle; running is jarring. Water exercise like aquafit is a good choice because the water cushions your body while also providing resistance to give you a good workout. I started doing aquafit during my first pregnancy and have enjoyed it on and off since then.

Other gentle exercise choices include biking, weights, and resistance machines. If all you can do is walk around the block (with a toddler in a stroller), then do that! Just getting out and being active will help both your mental and physical health as you prepare for baby.

If you've never exercised before, start carefully. Pick something that you are comfortable doing (e.g., if you hate water, don't go for aquafit). Don't push yourself too hard. Consult your doctor or midwife if you have any pain or concerns.

In your third trimester, pregnancy toning can help prepare key muscles for labour. Doula and birth coach Lori Bregman recommends specific exercises for each trimester in *The Mindful Mom-to-be.* I do squats during labour to help open my pelvis and often try to start doing these in my third trimester.

CHAPTER SIX

Eating Well for a Healthy Pregnancy

We've all heard the joke that pregnant women are eating for two. Before you let yourself eat whatever you want, however, remember that you aren't eating for two *adults*. While pregnant, you only need to increase your calorie intake by about 15 percent or 300 calories. That's equivalent to two granola bars or an English muffin with peanut butter and a banana.

Instead of eating more, try eating smaller meals with snacks in between—like your baby will when he or she is born.

Listen to your body telling you when you are hungry or not. If you aren't hungry, don't eat. If you are hungry, don't stuff yourself; eat slowly until you feel your body tell you that you've had enough. I kept a few granola bars in my office drawer or purse so I could snack as I needed to, which also helped stave off nausea.

> While pregnant, you only need to increase your calorie intake by about 15% or 300 calories.

Vitamins are an important part of a healthy pregnancy. Make sure you are taking a good multivitamin or prenatal vitamin. If you have questions about vitamins, ask your doctor or midwife for recommendations on what to take. One key ingredient in your vitamin should be folic acid, as this is crucial to your baby's developing brain. Some women find a whole foods supplement is easier on their stomachs than standard vitamins.

Eat breakfast. If morning sickness is a problem, try eating breakfast in bed. Have a piece of toast or a small muffin before you climb out of bed. This is a great opportunity for your spouse to pamper you! If that's not possible, however, plan ahead. You can put a granola bar or muffin on your nightstand when you go to bed and eat it before getting out of bed in the morning.

It's also important to get enough fiber in your diet. Keeping your system cleared out while you're producing waste for two people is essential. Anna knows all about this, as she gets really sick if she doesn't:

In all of my pregnancies but two, I've gotten a late-pregnancy condition called cholestasis. This means my body can't cope well with the toxins from baby and myself. Instead of being eliminated, these toxins end up under my skin.

Sounds fun, right? Just like getting chickenpox at Christmas. Especially when you're too itchy to sleep. So you see the importance of trying to prevent such a thing... but how?

The only really effective way I've found to keep my body regular and on track is to eat Kellogg's All-Bran Flakes every day. Yup, good old bran cereal has done more to keep me healthy than trying to eliminate sugar, fried fat, excess salt, etc., though those are important, too. My obstetrician suggested trying All-Bran Flakes in my third or fourth pregnancy. When I'm really faithful to it, I am much better. With my fourth baby, I didn't even get cholestasis at all.

The tricky bit is eating bran *every day*. A few times I went through most of the pregnancy healthy. Then when I got a bad cold or cough, I neglected my All-Bran Flakes for a few weeks. That was enough to do it; I got cholestasis again. And this condition is not only uncomfortable but increases the chance of stillbirth as your pregnancy progresses. I've experienced this. I don't wish it on anyone.

So that's why I thought I'd share this simple trick to keep up your bran, which clears out your gut and keeps your system running clean. This way you can be a safe environment for your baby to grow and develop.

Finally, coffee is a diuretic, so while some women choose to eliminate it in pregnancy, I find a cup in the morning also helps move things along. Besides me!

Pregnancy should be a time of excitement, not stress over what you're eating or how much you're exercising. Do focus on taking care of yourself and your baby but keep it simple.

CHAPTER SEVEN

Can You Drink Coffee and Tea while Pregnant?

I spent a lot of time reading tea labels when I was pregnant with Lily. I was often visiting my mother-in-law, and we'd decide we wanted a cup of tea. Then I'd rustle through the tins of tea in her cupboard, searching for one that fit our mood—and my pregnant state.

I've been surprised by how many of my friends offer me herbal tea instead of coffee when I'm pregnant. They're aware that caffeine isn't the greatest for baby, but don't realize some teas should be avoided too. Here's what I've learned about drinking coffee and tea in pregnancy.

Studies have shown that consuming too much caffeine during pregnancy can cause either miscarriage or low birth weights. Caffeine acts a stimulant, which increases your heart rate and metabolism—and your baby's. Too much of that can be bad for the baby.

However, one or two cups of coffee a day is okay. If you like more coffee, try switching to decaf instead.

Black, green, and oolong teas also contain caffeine, although not as much as coffee, so they should also be consumed in moderation. Green tea can prevent your body from absorbing folic acid and iron, which are important nutrients for pregnant moms. If you like green tea, try to avoid taking it at the same time as your multivitamin.

Herbal teas do not have caffeine, but herbs have their own medicinal properties.

If you have a favourite tea, ask your prenatal care provider if it's okay to keep drinking it. Herbs you may want to avoid include passion-flower, goldenseal, black and blue cohosh (unless recommended by your midwife to induce labour), hibiscus (a common ingredient in many teas), lemongrass, and evening primrose.

Teas that are helpful during pregnancy include ginger and mint teas, which may reduce morning sickness, and rooibos tea, which is caffeine-free and an antioxidant. You can also look for teas specifically for pregnant women.

In the end, it comes down to what you think is best for you and your baby. My first midwife recommended raspberry leaf to me for strengthening the uterus; other health experts advise avoiding raspberry leaf tea because it can cause uterine contractions and miscarriage. I've used raspberry leaf tea with most of my pregnancies without any problems. If you have concerns or a history of miscarriage, you'll want to avoid it.

Personally, I prefer coffee over tea, but I'll still limit myself to a cup a day—and keep reading tea labels.

CHAPTER EIGHT

Weird Things that Happen When You're Pregnant

Everyone knows about pregnancy cravings. They're one of the weird things that happen when you're pregnant. During my first pregnancy, I was often asked if I'd had any cravings yet. But there are a lot of other strange symptoms to pregnancy too.

Here's my list of weird things that (may or may not) happen when you're pregnant. Some of these come from my own experience and some from friends' experiences. Just remember that every woman experiences pregnancy (and birth and motherhood!) in her own unique way.

1. Exhaustion

This is probably the biggest symptom of pregnancy; it starts the soonest and lasts the longest. I'm surprised the most by first trimester exhaustion. I mean, the baby is at this point the size of a bean; how can such a tiny being make me so tired?

I understand that the third trimester is going to be tiring because you're carrying so much extra weight. For many women, the exhaustion starts early in the pregnancy and doesn't end until… well, maybe until the baby heads off to college.

For many women, the exhaustion starts early in the pregnancy and doesn't end until… well, maybe until the baby heads off to college.

2. Food aversions

There are pregnancy cravings and then there are pregnancy aversions. Some friends of mine can't drink coffee when pregnant. Another friend of mine couldn't stand the smell of red meat cooking during her pregnancy; her poor husband ate out a lot (or barbequed outside when she wasn't home).

I haven't been able to eat wraps since I was pregnant with Sunshine. That made more sense once I found out I wasn't supposed to eat cold cuts during pregnancy, but other aversions may not make sense. Some things you loved you'll now hate. (Hopefully it ends with the pregnancy!)

3. Breakouts

Ugh. You think you're over this when you leave the teenage years behind, but nope, pregnancy plays as much havoc with your hormones as puberty does.

You may find that the breakouts and acne continue into the first few months after baby's birth as well, as your hormones continue to fluctuate. My face has often driven me nuts during my pregnancies. Keep using your cleanser and toner and resort to some make-up if you need it.

4. Swelling

Thankfully, I haven't experienced this. One friend of mine, however, had to get her wedding rings cut off because her hands were so swollen. Other friends complain about "cankles" and how much their legs swell during pregnancy.

Pregnancy books will offer much advice on preventing this. The reality is that your body is dealing with a lot of things during this time, including producing extra blood for you and the baby. Some of it will settle in your legs or hands. Pay attention to your rings to prevent costly measures!

5. Forgetfulness

What was I going to say? Oh right… mommy brain is real. You're growing a baby and that takes a lot of work, so go with it. Sometimes you'll forget where your keys are or why you walked into the room.

Organization and routines can help, as can lots of prayer to St. Anthony for things you've lost. Otherwise, all you can do is keep a good sense of humour and hope you remember it eventually.

I'd like to promise that this will go away with your pregnancy like the swelling, but… it'll probably stick around like the exhaustion.

6. Varicose Veins

Varicose veins are actually related to hemorrhoids (another problem which may plague you before or after birth). Many of my friends have experienced these bulging, painful veins during pregnancy. During pregnancy, they are hard to treat with conventional methods, but they usually go away once the baby arrives.

Massaging your legs with essential oils may help to increase circulation and decrease varicose veins.

Some women experience other symptoms, like a heightened sense of smell or a change in their hair. Of course, if you have any questions or concerns about anything you're experiencing during your pregnancy, you should talk to your doctor or midwife.

CHAPTER NINE

How to Survive First-Trimester Exhaustion

With my fourth pregnancy, my morning sickness began at six weeks—exhaustion and nausea but no vomiting. I was a bit surprised. I've had morning sickness with all of my pregnancies, so I knew to expect it. What surprised me was how early it started.

My husband and I had just barely begun talking about the fact that we were pregnant again. The baby was not even the size of a bean, but already, he or she was making huge changes within my body.

Today, fingernails are developing, or maybe brain cells. My body is putting all its energy into knitting together a knee.

With all but my first pregnancy, I took Diclectin (a Canadian morning sickness medication) to treat my pregnancy nausea. While Diclectin helps take away most of the yucky feelings, it doesn't help much with the exhaustion. I would go to bed at eight or nine pm, leaving my husband to study (or do the grocery shopping, which he likes doing better than I do anyway).

Many mornings, I slept in, one ear open to my older girls playing with their dolls or ponies. Thankfully, Sunshine and Lily were old enough during my fourth pregnancy that they could help themselves to breakfast and entertain their younger sisters. All the girls are also good at playing by themselves.

However, I struggled with the feeling that I was doing nothing. I'm a to-do-list person. For me, a good day is when I can say that I accomplished a lot. I cleaned house, did the girls' schoolwork, wrote some blog posts, took the girls to the park, made supper, called a friend, baked some cookies, etc.

During my first trimester, I struggled to get one of those things done in a day. Homeschooling was a priority, obviously, but there were days when all we did was math.

I tried to remind myself that I was growing a baby. *Today, fingernails are developing, or maybe brain cells. My body is putting all its energy into knitting together a knee.*

However, that's an unseen thing. I can't exactly check "made an eyebrow" off my to-do list. Especially when my husband came home to a messy house after I'd called him to ask him to pick up supper on his way home. He'd ask, "What did you do today?" Um, I had a nap in a desperate attempt to stay awake past the girls' bedtime so we can have some time together.

I'm jealous of my friends who fly through their pregnancies with hardly any nausea or tiredness. Yet other friends, who would desperately love to be pregnant, remind me to be grateful for this tiny life inside me and to slow down and enjoy this time, even with all its discomfort. My little girls remind me that pregnancy is soon over and well worth the fun and joys that come after.

For nine short months, I'm privileged to carry another life inside me—a precious, beautiful, growing little baby whose very being rocks mine even when he or she is only a few weeks old. So this is what I remind myself during first-trimester exhaustion:

Give yourself grace. This will pass, in time. Listen to your body and slow down as you need to (and can) and focus on the miracle happening inside your womb.

Prioritize. What really needs to get done today? What can wait for tomorrow (or next week)?

Ask for help. Your husband may have to pitch in a bit more, or your kids. Maybe a friend can watch the kids for a bit so you can rest.

Maybe you can afford to hire a house cleaner once or twice or order in meals a bit more during these months.

Find quiet, restful things you can do with your kids so they still feel included. Maybe you can read novels to them, do a puzzle together, or colour. Perhaps Daddy can grab some books at the library for you, or Grandma can send over some new colouring books and markers.

Nap if you can or get to bed early. Again, remember this is just for a few months. I let the girls watch a movie while I tried to rest even though I don't like relying on the TV. When my energy returned, we cut down on screen time again. An alternative to the TV was letting the girls play educational games on my electronic tablet.

Take advantage of bursts of energy. Don't overdo it, but maybe that means getting a meal together or the house tidied, or going on an outing with the family for a bit.

Try to eat foods high in iron and check with your healthcare provider about your iron levels. I often have low iron, especially during pregnancy, which doesn't help my energy levels. Taking an iron supplement and eating iron-rich foods can help.

Be realistic about what you can and can't do and communicate that to your husband and your family. My husband likes getting out as a family to do things on the weekend, but I had to warn him I could probably only go for an hour or so before I'd be crashing (and getting grumpy). Or I'd try to have a nap while he did something with the girls for a bit so we could do something else later as a family.

CHAPTER TEN

When You Don't Want to be Pregnant

For a long time, it was hard for me to understand why a woman wouldn't want to be pregnant. For as long as I can remember, I've wanted to be a mom. When my husband and I got married, we knew we wanted a big family. My husband had joked about a honeymoon baby during our engagement, and that's exactly what we had.

Our first three babies were neither planned nor unplanned. By worldly standards, we shouldn't have even been getting pregnant. Our honeymoon baby was conceived while we were living on my salary and my husband was finishing his education degree. She was born during his first teaching practicum.

Lily was conceived just after we'd moved to a new town. My husband and I were both job hunting. I managed to work enough during my pregnancy to qualify for maternity leave. That helped pay for our expenses when we went back to school immediately after her birth.

Jade was born in our third year of university. I felt a few concerns about having a new baby while both of us were trying to finish our degrees, but I wasn't really too worried about it. We'd always managed a new baby before, even when the circumstances weren't the greatest. And so we fit Jade into our lives too (hand-me-downs from the older girls certainly helped!).

I actually planned to get pregnant with Pearl. My husband and I had finished our degrees. He was working a new job—his first steady, full-time, permanent (we thought) job with good benefits. We were renting a nice house and we had a supportive community around us. It was a good time to have a baby—or so I thought.

Nine months later, my husband faced a lot of stress at work. I dealt with some depression after Pearl's birth, as she was a colicky baby who screamed a lot. As she got older, I felt like four was a nice number of kids for our family. If we had another baby, I decided, it would be after a big gap—maybe three or four years away.

So when I found out I was expecting Joey, I wasn't happy. Like all my other pregnancies, I had a feeling I was pregnant for several days before I took the test. One night, as I was driving our babysitter home, my husband suggested I grab a bottle of wine on the way back. Instead, I stopped by the drug store for a pregnancy test.

Standing in our bathroom, waiting for the test results, I hoped I was wrong about this feeling. As the lines spread across the stick, a sick feeling settled in my stomach. No. Not another pregnancy. I wasn't ready for a baby again.

> I yelled at God, because I didn't want to be pregnant and they did and how was that even fair? Why would He let this happen?

And this wasn't a good time to be pregnant. I ticked off the reasons in my head. My husband had recently been laid off from that job he planned to work until retirement. Our marriage was on the rocks (again). The baby would be due in December, which meant we wouldn't be going back to Alberta for Christmas with our families. We'd just bought annual ski passes for our local ski hill, but a new baby would make skiing difficult.

I wanted to curl up in a ball and cry. I wanted to go back in time and change that night we ignored the fertility app on my phone. I felt guilty about my feelings because I have a lot of friends who've struggled to conceive or had multiple miscarriages. Then I yelled at God because I didn't want to be pregnant and they did and how was that even fair? Why would He let this happen?

For a month, I dealt with depression and negativity as I thought about this new little life in my tummy. I didn't want to face morning sickness, much less labour pain. I didn't want the inconvenience I knew a new baby would bring to our lives. Again and again, I thought about all the problems this baby would cause. How were we were going to fit a fifth child into our three-bedroom condo or our seven-seater minivan?

What changed my perspective on my pregnancy were my daughters and my mom friends. All of them were excited when I told them about the new baby. My daughters didn't know about the stress of Daddy's job loss, or the fear of labour, or the other things I worried about. They just knew that a new baby was fun and exciting and happening soon.

Pregnancy comes with a lot of emotions. They may be positive, exciting emotions, or negative, despairing emotions, or a mix of all.

My friends were equally supportive. Many of my friends have six or eight or ten kids. They asked if we needed anything. I said yes, because I'd started giving away baby and maternity clothing after Pearl.

I decided, because I needed something different, to have the twenty-week ultrasound with this pregnancy. I didn't want to wait until baby's birth to find out if "it" was a he or she. I needed something different, something positive to hang onto. I also needed to know whether to start collecting boy or girl clothes from friends who offered!

Seeing my baby moving, kicking and squirming on the black-and-white screen, was truly special and unique.

We found out baby was a boy, which was different after having four girls. It wasn't that we'd been hoping for a boy (I would have been happy to stay a #girlmom). It meant that I could get new everything for this baby, without guilt, and that was like being a first-time mom again, with all the excitement around it. Out with the worn-out pink and purple, in with the brand-new blue and grey.

And as I'd discovered with my first four babies, I don't know what's going to happen nine months down the road. My husband spent more than six months job hunting. Just before our son was born, he accepted a job near us that offered a flexible schedule.

He was able to take Friday afternoons off so we could go up to the ski hill as a family. We took turns watching our youngest two kids in the lodge and chasing the older three kids down the ski runs. We didn't go home for Christmas, but my mom came to help for the first week after Joey's birth, just before the holidays.

Joey was a colicky baby, just like Pearl. At ten months, he was still waking up multiple times a night, just like all my girls. I still tried to accomplish too much on my to-do list. And we found reasons to laugh and smile with the baby. The girls delighted in their new brother, and I worked to appreciate his cute moments and let go of the fussy moments.

Pregnancy comes with a lot of emotions. They may be positive, exciting emotions or negative, despairing emotions, or a mix of all. Your emotions may go up and down and change frequently throughout your pregnancy. I encourage you to journal them, pray about them, and talk to your friends, priest, or counselor about them.

CHAPTER ELEVEN

Let's Talk about Miscarriage

It is not a nice thing to talk about the possibility of loss in a book for expectant moms, who are filled with hope and wonder at the new life inside themselves. It is not nice, but it is necessary, for loss is all too common, even though it is often endured in silence.

Personally, I knew nothing of miscarriage until my sixth pregnancy. I didn't know what to say to people who had lost their babies, or how to support them. I was hesitant to bring up their grief in case it made it hurt even more.

But when my world was torn apart by losing my daughter Josephine due to a cord accident in labour, I learned that such a loss should not be endured alone. I reached out by writing poetry about my sorrow. In sharing my pain, I discovered that so many other brave mamas existed.

To be open to life is to be open to death. This is the reality of our frail human existence, which is ultimately a gift.

Their love, support and wisdom helped me endure the worst and to keep hoping to find happiness again. Their example gave me courage to have two rainbow babies after I had little Jo, even though it felt terrifying to risk losing again.

To be open to life is to be open to death. This is the reality of our frail human existence, which is ultimately a gift.

Try to appreciate each day you have with the child in your womb, your love incarnate, your heart with its own heartbeat. Your lives will be forever linked, no matter what happens.

Someone once told me that because of blood crossover from the placenta into the mother's bloodstream, your baby's DNA mingles with your own and becomes forever a part of you. You are together, body and spirit, no matter what happens.

If you should suffer losing your little one, no matter how early or late in the pregnancy, know that your loss matters, and that your deep grief is a sign of your deep love. Reach out and seek support from a friend who has been through loss, from an online or in-person support group, or a counselor or priest who can help journey with you towards healing.

There are resources such as Elizabeth Ministries, run by parents who have experienced loss, who will come visit you at home to talk about your child. Sharing Magazine is a beautiful online magazine with stories from other bereaved parents who give their best advice on recovery after loss and on honouring your child, who will matter forever.

Lastly, please don't blame yourself. Don't play the "what if" or "if only" game. Sometimes miscarriages have a medical explanation; sometimes they don't and that is hard to accept. Babies aren't an item guaranteed to arrive or get your money back. They are a mystery and a miracle.

However, there are resources to help you, such as recurring miscarriage clinics at the hospital, herbal tea cleanses to strengthen your reproductive system, and even acupuncture. There are doctors who specialize in NAPRO technology and natural family planning methods like Creighton (which helps you track your natural signs of fertility and understand your cycle better so you can achieve and support a healthy pregnancy).

I wish you all safe and happy pregnancies and births, and may you never need any of the advice above!

CHAPTER TWELVE

Pregnancy after Baby Loss

Expecting a baby after losing one is hard. Beautiful but hard. The thing is that you don't really expect a baby in the same way—you hope for one, and it is a fragile hope.

I'm normally one to be on the phone with mom buddies the second the little plus sign shows up on the pregnancy test. After I lost my daughter Josephine, I became more hesitant to talk about things early on. My usual excitement was tempered by the confusing feelings of having lost my last child and not knowing how to feel a simple, trusting hope that everything would be fine.

I did still hope and trust, but in a more complex and nuanced way. Not in the way of thinking things would always turn out how I wanted them to, but in hoping in a plan that's bigger than mine, a vision far wiser and more encompassing than mine…. in a love stronger than death, knowing that no matter what, I can never truly be separated from my babies.

Sometimes children are so wise. My five-year-old once told me, "Don't worry, Mummy. Either the new baby will come be with us, or he will go be with Josephine in Heaven. So it's okay." What strength and clarity of vision!

It was hard to take this risk again—the risk that I might not see my baby smile or breathe until I met him in Heaven—but it was a way of affirming that I was still alive, still had hope, still believed in goodness in a world where hard things also happen.

Besides, the only way to ensure my heart could never be broken again would be to stop it pumping, but risking brokenness is essential to being open to life and to love. It's part of the fragile thing called being human.

Several of my close friends have lost babies and have been able to have another baby safely after. Those babies are a beacon of hope for me.

I rejoice in each one of them. I realize they are miracles and a free gift rather than a right.

We think we have so many rights, but we forget that people can only come to us as gift, in the freedom of love.

I also rejoice in the children I do have, just seeing them running around full of life, dancing and laughing, and I think to myself, "They made it. That incredible journey… like little travelers from a far off planet, they made it through the epic journey of the few inches from womb to world and arrived home."

I pray for all of you, that your little ones may arrive safely into their mama's arms, and that this time, your tears will be of joy. I have now been greatly blessed with two rainbow babies after losing my daughter, one little boy and then, bittersweet, a little girl.

Keep up your hope, courageous mamas!

Second Trimester

Have you had the chance to do much art lately?
I ask my artist friend as she chats
confidentially with her toddler on her lap,
which is blossoming with baby belly
under her bright pink shirt.

Not too much, she replies.
Just surviving and getting ready for baby,
but looking forward to nursing
as a time for inspiration.
Yeah, I reply, it's that quiet contemplative time
that is the source of inspiration for sure.
An openness to the divine, she replies,
that's where art comes from.

I want to tell her that right now
she is cooperating with
the most divine creation there is—
that of a human life—
the artistic triumph of the world,
a piece of art that is by its very nature immortal
but I get interrupted by
one of my kids who needs a new towel.

So I can't tell her she is weaving
with sinews of love
painting with brushstrokes of hope
writing with stories strung on
tiny ropes of DNA
forging new paths for faithfulness
strengthening family bonds
with tiny bricks of beauty
cells diverse and unique
splendidly forming into
a new child of promise.

~ Anna Eastland

CHAPTER THIRTEEN

How to Choose a Name for Your Little One

We were only a few months pregnant with Sunshine when we spent an hour discussing baby names while driving. By the time we got home, we'd chosen two possible sets of names for the baby. I was a bit surprised we managed to find names we both liked so quickly. Some of our other decisions as newlyweds had taken much more talking.

Choosing names for our subsequent babies got more difficult. We still had the boy's name we liked when we were picking names for Sunshine, but we disagreed on middle names.

As for girls' names… we seemed to go around and around. One night before our second daughter was born, we visited my in-laws and the conversation revolved around baby names for several hours. We talked about this relative's name and what this person named their kids and can you believe someone would pick a name like this and did you know that Great-Grandpa's middle name was…

It's a hard job, to choose a name your child will have for the rest of their lives. Your personal preferences will impact your choices, as well as other people you've met with certain names. One of my girlfriends told me that her favourite name was Josiah—until she had not one but three Josiahs in the first Grade 5 class she taught as a new teacher, and they were *all* little terrors.

I don't like names that can be either a boys' name or a girls' name. I want people to know, just by looking at her name, that she's a girl. (Even when Sunshine was clad entirely in pink, I still got the question "Boy or girl?" so maybe the name isn't so important either).

I don't like names that are too short or names that are too long.

I don't want a name that's too uncommon or one that is too common (nothing on the top ten girls' names charts). I really debated our oldest daughter's name, as I liked it, but it was very popular during my generation. However, she's the only girl we've met in *her* generation with her name.

There are a lot of names that just don't go with our last name (but make for some good jokes). We joke about Noah Way (no way!) and Heidi Way (hideaway) and others, but we wouldn't use them.

I want a name that has some meaning, something our child can be proud of when asked why that's her name. So I don't mind using family names; Sunshine is named after both of her grandmothers as well as after her spiritual mother, Mary. Both my brothers were named for their grandfather, and my son is also named for his grandfathers.

We like choosing saint names for our children. Lily's name was inspired by two saints—one was a mother of eight children and the other is a patron saint of midwives. When I was stressed about where I was giving birth and who was catching the baby, I figured those saints would be great intercessors.

Pearl is named for St. Margaret of Scotland, whose feast day is her birthday. My second and third babies were both born late, so when I realized Pearl's due date was St. Margaret's feast day, I began asking her intercession for a safe, timely birth. St. Margaret was the mother of eight children, so I felt sure she knew what it was like to anticipate a baby's arrival! And whether it was St. Margaret's intercession or all the dates I ate during Pearl's pregnancy, Pearl arrived right on time.

> I want a name that has some meaning, something our child can be proud of when asked why that's her name.

My husband likes joking about outrageous names for our babies. There are plenty of obscure saints with hard-to-pronounce names, so he suggests St. Grwst or St. Wunibald. Or he'd say, "What about Johann?" and I'd say, "We're not Swiss." Have fun with the naming process but recognize when your partner is joking and when they aren't (and respect their serious suggestions).

45

Experts also recommend looking at what initials your baby will have if you choose certain name combinations. We've avoided names starting with vowels for our kids' middle names, as it would be too easy to give them the initials JAW or MEW. If Jade had been a boy, the names we liked would have given him the initials LAW. As my husband was in law school at the time, we thought it was funny—but maybe it was a good thing she was a girl instead.

We have friends who find out their baby's gender at twenty weeks and then share their baby's name. Other friends refuse to even discuss baby names until they see their new son or daughter. We've usually picked names well before baby arrives, but we don't share those names until baby's birth. Discuss with your spouse what you'd like to do and respect each other's ideas (and family traditions) around this.

Our fifth baby was the first whose gender we found out before he was born. I liked knowing him as "him" instead of "it," and mentally named him. While we still didn't share his name until his birth, I enjoyed this time to practice it quietly and get used to it.

You may find inspiration for baby names in your cultural background, spiritual traditions, or family tree. You can browse baby name books at the library or just watch for names around you. (One of my friends found her daughter's name in the credits rolling at the end of a movie!)

Pray and think about the names you choose and use this time to draw closer to your spouse. Respect each other's ideas and the feelings that go along with various names suggested. I've always liked Rachel, but my husband didn't like a character by that name on the TV show *Friends* (which I've never seen), so we haven't used it. You'll both be calling this child by that name for a long time, and you need to like it!

CHAPTER FOURTEEN

Top 3 Questions You May Hear

When I was pregnant with my first baby, I was surprised by how many strangers commented on the state of my belly. Women I'd never met wanted to touch my pregnant tummy and know when my due date was.

After having five babies, I've gotten used to this phenomenon (though as an introvert, I still don't understand why complete strangers would ask me questions I'd never ask my friends!).

Enjoy your first trimester of pregnancy, while your baby is still hiding and only those whom you choose to share this information with know about him or her. Once your tummy begins to reveal your state, be prepared for the intrusion of curious strangers.

Here are the top three questions I've been asked over the course of my five pregnancies:

1. "How are you feeling?"

I heard this question a few times a day, especially as more people knew about my pregnancy. Everyone knows of morning sickness, so that's the first thing they think of when they hear about your pregnancy or notice your belly.

This question came most frequently from co-workers or friends. Feel free to be honest with them about how you're doing and whether they can help. Your friends who've been pregnant before may be able to share some tips about what helped them deal with morning sickness, body changes, emotions, and more.

2. "Have you had any weird cravings?"

A pregnant woman is notorious for craving weird things. One friend told me her doctor advised her to indulge any craving except for those that weren't edible, such as dirt or laundry detergent.

Those who are curious about this during my first pregnancy were disappointed to hear I didn't have any cravings at all. In my second pregnancy, I craved fast-food burgers. I worked at Starbucks and often packed myself a lunch. However, I'd get to my break, look at my packed lunch, and then head to the nearest burger chain.

Another friend of ours told us her husband was disappointed she had no cravings because he was ready for the midnight dash for ice cream and pickles.

If you are having cravings for certain foods, this is something your husband can share in. My hubby has always been happy to indulge my cravings for burgers!

3. "Are you going to find out what you're having?"

This is probably the most common question I've gotten, over all five pregnancies. Because modern technology has given mankind the ability (sometimes) to find out what sex baby is while in utero, everyone wants to know.

One of my coworkers told everyone her baby's sex and name months before the baby was born. By contrast, we didn't find out our baby's gender for our first four pregnancies. Friends of ours told us that the surprise was better, so we waited.

If you're quick-witted, you can have fun when people ask, "What are you having?" My husband likes to say, "A human." One of his friends, who already had two daughters, liked to joke, "Well, we're hoping for a puppy!"

Everyone will have a story for you about this and why you should or shouldn't find out your baby's gender. Whether you find out your baby's gender, and whether you choose to share that, is up to you and your husband. Make sure you discuss this with each other and agree on what you're doing. Then plan your cheeky or polite answer when strangers ask the question.

CHAPTER FIFTEEN

My Non-Maternity Maternity Wardrobe

Being on my fourth pregnancy should have meant I had lots of maternity clothes (and everything else I needed for baby). However, when I pulled down my box of maternity clothes, I found myself putting most of them back up in the closet.

There were the dress shirts I wore when I worked in an office during Sunshine's pregnancy and never put on again. There were the black pants and tops I wore when I worked in Starbucks during Lily's pregnancy and never put on again. There were the baggy T-shirts I wore when I was a student not bound by a dress code during Jade's pregnancy and never put on again.

So for the first thirty weeks of my last two pregnancies, I found myself being creative with my regular clothes and wearing mostly non-maternity outfits.

I'm sure I'm not the only mom who's faced this dilemma about what to wear with a burgeoning belly, so I thought I'd share some pictures of what's worked for me.

For clothes that last longer than nine months, look for:

- pants or shorts with a low waist or elastic waist band that fits on your hips
- long shirts with extra stretch or flare
- shirts with a high waist
- tops and bottoms that mix and match well

Dresses are also good as you don't need to worry about the waist. Look for longer dresses that gather about your bust and then flow loosely from there. I've seen lots of cute maxi dresses that work well on pregnant forms (without looking like shapeless muumuus!).

Leggings can also be comfortable during pregnancy as they offer you more stretch.

What about maternity underwear? I've never bought any. Again, look for underwear that is comfortable and practical. Most stores sell ladies' briefs that will fit under your pregnant belly.

Another option is to exchange maternity wear with friends. At my mom's group, we've passed around several tops and dresses during our pregnancies. Pants are harder to share as they fit differently, but a dress is more forgiving. I've joked with my friends that we have a "Sisterhood of the Traveling Maternity Dress," but it works.

And finally… if you completely hate your maternity clothing after wearing those pieces (and only those pieces) for nine months straight, that's okay! Give it to a friend or donate it to an organization that helps moms in need.

Even if you save your pregnancy wardrobe for your next pregnancy, elastics tend to wear out in storage and (like me!) you may not like those clothes anymore in two years than you do now.

Why it works: I love this tank top because it's soft, drapey, long, and has lots of stretch. The skirt has an elastic waistband, which I simply wore around my hips rather than at my waist.

Why it works: This tank top is more fitted but long enough to go around my belly. The skirt is the same as the purple skirt above (if it works, buy it in all colours!) and these two outfits can be mixed-and-matched too if I don't want to be monochromatic.

Why it works: This top does fit skinny but has lots of length and stretch so I've been able to keep wearing it as my belly bulges. The shorts are low-waisted and have a tied waist belt so I can adjust them as needed.

Why it works: I've had this top since I was pregnant with Sunshine. High-waisted tops were in style and work well with a pregnant tummy. This top also has good stretch. The capris have a slightly higher waist and are now a bit tight, but I just roll the waistband under my tummy.

Why it works: Okay, sometimes I still resort to the baggy T-shirt. The capris are among my favourite whether I'm pregnant or not; because they are low-waisted, I've been able to keep wearing them (as long as I pair them with a long shirt).

CHAPTER SIXTEEN

Tips for Dealing with Prenatal Backaches

Back aches are common during the last half of pregnancy and may continue into your first few months postpartum. The growing weight of the baby in your tummy causes understandable strain on your back muscles. This pain can also cause poor sleep and worsen the exhaustion you're already feeling towards the end of your pregnancy.

My favourite way of dealing with back aches during pregnancy is a hot water bottle or a microwaveable heat pad. I'll prop the heating pad behind me in a comfy chair or take it to bed with me at night. The heat usually works fairly quickly to ease my back pain.

Often, my back starts aching because I've been doing one activity for too long. For example, maybe I've spent the day sitting in my chair blogging and homeschooling. My upper back usually begins to ache after a few hours, prompting me to move.

Other times, if we've been out all day, my lower back will ache, letting me know I need to sit down and take it easy.

Pause to take note of what causes your back ache and see if a change in position will help it go away. If you work in a job that requires sitting or standing all day, you may have to be more creative about changing position. Whether you are sitting or standing, you can also watch your posture (don't slouch).

When I was pregnant with Sunshine, I brought an exercise ball to my office. The ball helped me maintain posture and move a little bit even while sitting, preventing back pain. Some offices offer standing work stations, so you can raise or lower your desk to change your position.

When I was pregnant with Lily, I worked at a coffee shop as a barista. I made sure to sit during my breaks. Cleaning or restocking let me squat, kneel, and move about in other ways that helped prevent back pain. You can also talk to your supervisor about using a stool or chair if you are going to be in one area (such as the cash register) for long periods.

I haven't gotten a massage while pregnant, but this made a huge difference for me with postpartum back aches. (Yes, some aches and pains of pregnancy continue into the "fourth" trimester.) Ask your doctor or midwife if they can recommend a masseuse who specializes in pregnant patients.

You may be able to get your health insurance to cover your massage. Check with your insurance provider before booking your massage to see if you need a note from your doctor or midwife. You'll also want to make sure you are seeing a registered massage therapist (RMT).

If you can't get away for a massage, sign up for the MELT: Massage for Couples courses online and use this time to bond with your hubby! It'll give him something to do to help you and allow him to feel more involved with your pregnancy.

Pause to take note of what causes your back ache and see if a change in position will help it go away.

I avoid over-the-counter remedies when pregnant, but many homeopathic remedies are safe to take. For back pain, I've been taking arnica, which is also available as a gel or ointment (if you have someone who can rub your back for you).

The National Center for Homeopathy also suggests sepia and other remedies, depending on the type of back pain you are experiencing. If you've never tried homeopathic remedies or aren't sure which one is right for your back pain, see a homeopath or naturopath.

Soaking in a hot aromatherapy bath can also help with muscle soreness. *1001 Natural Remedies* suggests adding five drops each of marjoram, rosemary and lavender essential oils to two cups Epsom salts.

The authors explain, "Epsom salts promote relaxation, marjoram helps relieve pain and is deeply relaxing; rosemary eases muscle stiffness; and lavender is both a mild antispasmodic and gentle sedative." This can be a great way to relax and ease back pain at the end of the day, so you get a better night's sleep.

Exercise can help prevent back pain by strengthening your back muscles. If you exercised regularly before getting pregnant, you can probably continue your exercise routine well into your pregnancy. (Check with your health care provider if you have any questions or concerns.)

If you haven't exercised until now, choose a gentle exercise (such as swimming or aquafit) or a pre-natal exercise class and ease yourself into the exercise. In *The Mindful Mom-to-be,* doula Lori Bregman suggests month-by-month exercises to help with the various needs of your body throughout your pregnancy.

This is another chance to listen to your body. Don't ignore your back pain or try to push through it. Take note of how and when your back hurts and what helps to relieve that pain. Your body is working hard to grow a baby, and you need to take care of both yourself and baby during this time.

CHAPTER SEVENTEEN

Natural Ways to Strengthen Your Uterus

In the previous chapters, we've shared about improving your pregnancy and preparing for labour by eating well, exercising, and learning. Some of these can seem overwhelming at times (there are definitely days when I don't want to hit the gym, much less hit the gym with a bulging belly).

Red raspberry leaf tea, evening primrose oil, and dates are all said to strengthen a women's uterus. Two of these I've used sporadically with all my pregnancies; one I heard about only with my fourth pregnancy. Together, all three helped me have my best labour and recovery with my fourth and fifth babies.

Red Raspberry Leaf Tea

My midwives recommended red raspberry leaf tea to me during my pregnancy with Sunshine. Raspberry leaf tea has been used medicinally for thousands of years as a uterine tonic. It contains several good nutrients like Vitamin B complex, calcium, iron, and magnesium. This herb is also said to lower blood sugar and blood pressure, improve your immune system and circulation, and ease morning sickness.

I found red raspberry leaf tea at my local health food store. Check boxes carefully before buying; not all teas labelled "raspberry tea" are actually red raspberry leaf tea. Some are just raspberry flavored.

I drank a cup a day for most of my pregnancy and increased it to two or three cups for the last couple of weeks before my due date.

BellyBelly.com.au notes that "Studies have shown that women who take red raspberry leaf have a reduced incidence of birth interventions. Research has also found that women who drink red raspberry leaf tea regularly towards the end of their pregnancies had shorter second stages of labour than those who don't."

Red raspberry leaf tea can increase the strength or frequency of Braxton-Hicks contractions. If you have complications during pregnancy or a history of early labour, it's best to avoid it.

Evening Primrose Oil

I took evening primrose oil towards the end of my pregnancy with Jade (especially once my due date passed). It's usually available in the supplements section of your grocery store or at natural health food stores.

Anna takes evening primrose oil from the first trimester onwards to help with emotional balance. When I asked my midwives about it, they approved it, in small doses for the first two trimesters and then increasing my dose after thirty-six weeks to prepare for labour.

There are few studies on evening primrose oil and conflicting information online. It acts as a prostaglandin that helps ripen the cervix before labour. It's also a source of essential fatty acids and omega-6 fatty acids.

Dates

During my fourth pregnancy, I saw a photo on Pinterest claiming dates helped with labour. Right away, I was intrigued. I like dates and, unlike the above options, they are a common food that surely couldn't have any concerns or side effects associated with them.

Looking into dates, I found there's a study published in the *Journal of Obstetrics and Gynaecology* proving dates do have advantages for pregnancy. Dates seem to mimic the hormone oxytocin and made it less likely for women to require medication to start labour or help it progress. Dates are a good source of fiber, iron, folate, Vitamin K, magnesium, and potassium.

The recommendation is to eat six dates daily during pregnancy but especially during the last trimester. Dates are available in several forms in your grocery store—fresh, dried, etc—and can be easily used in baking or cooking.

Add them to your cereal in the morning, or to a bowl of yogurt and fruit, or have them for an afternoon snack when you need an energy boost. Matrimonial bars (also known as date squares) are another yummy option.

Do these work?

Do these natural ways to prepare your body for labour really work? I can't remember exactly when I started taking each of these in my fourth pregnancy, but by my third trimester I was having each one daily.

Pearl was born exactly on her due date (even though Lily and Jade were born a week and two weeks after their due dates, respectively). Her labour was roughly two hours shorter than any of my other three labours (eight instead of ten hours). My postpartum bleeding and cramping seemed to be less than with my last births (despite friends assuring me that afterbirth pains get worse with each baby).

I used red raspberry leaf tea, evening primrose oil, and dates again during my fifth pregnancy. Joey was born only a couple days after his due date. His labour was my shortest (only six hours). Overall, comparing my five pregnancies, I think these three things did help me with my last two.

I recommend talking to your doctor or midwife before taking supplements or changing your diet during your pregnancy. My midwives recommended or were on board with these, but doctors may be a bit more dubious.

Do your research (as I did) and make a decision based on your own intuition and circumstances. If you have any complications or concerns during your pregnancy, you may want to avoid the tea and supplements.

Third Trimester

Tiny traveler
from the realm of inner space,
you float suspended
in dark warm liquid
upside down
untouched by gravity
tethered by a lifeline
to the mothership.
Outside, tiny blue rivers
run in veins over the rolling horizon.
Your world curves around you
like a constant embrace,
the pulse of your universe
beats reassuringly in your ears.
When you are launched into the outer world
in an epic one-foot journey–
"One small step for mankind"–
you enter a new solar system
where bright light abounds,
but the starlight from your former home
forever twinkles in your eyes.
Tiny traveler,
welcome to the world!

~ Anna Eastland

CHAPTER EIGHTEEN

Overcoming Prenatal Insomnia

Third trimester often signals the return of the exhaustion you faced during your first trimester. However, this time the exhaustion comes with a new problem: insomnia.

Your growing belly can make it hard to find a comfortable position in bed, even when you're so tired you think you could fall asleep standing up. Hours of tossing and turning with various pregnancies have taught me a few tricks.

White noise is something I've used for myself as often as for my babies. There are a variety of white noise machines available as well as free apps you can install on your phone or tablet. I like the ocean sound on the White Noise Baby app, which has a nice rhythm that often helps calm my racing thoughts. Most apps and white noise devices have multiple settings and sounds, so play with them until you find what works for you.

Essential oils are another relaxing strategy that is safe to use during pregnancy. Lavender is one of my favourite scents, either to diffuse while I fall asleep or just to apply topically (usually to my feet). You can also add lavender to a relaxing warm bath at the end of the day. Rose, Roman chamomile and other essential oils may be effective as well. (For more information, see my list of recommended resources.)

If you're dealing with anxiety or emotions around your pregnancy, writing them down can help you process what's going on and let it go.

I've often found that journaling at the end of the day helped me relax. If you're dealing with anxiety or emotions around your pregnancy, writing them down can help you process what's going on and let it go. Or this can be a good way just to go over the day and prevent your brain from constantly rehashing the day's events while you're trying to sleep.

Prayer and Bible or devotional reading also help. I kept my Bible, rosary, and a favourite devotional book near my bed. If I couldn't fall asleep, I'd turn on a low light and pick one to read. I found a deeper connection with Mary, as mother of Jesus, during my pregnancies. I reread the Nativity story, contemplating what she experienced, and asking for her intercession.

Avoid TVs and computers before bed. My husband and I enjoy watching movies and TV shows together, but I find that if I do this right before bed, it often keeps me awake. My mind wants to process what happened in the show or movie. The light from TV and computer screens may also affect our sleep patterns. Try to find other ways to relax and spend time with your husband at the end of the day, such as playing a board game, reading together, going for a walk, etc.

A body pillow can help support your growing tummy and make you more comfortable during this time. Friends of ours gave me a body pillow when I was pregnant with Sunshine, which I used for my next several pregnancies. Research online or visit your nearest baby store to see what they have.

Some prenatal body pillows can also be used as nursing pillows or baby supports after your pregnancy. While a pillow may seem expensive (especially if you just use it during your pregnancy), remember that your sleep is valuable. A well-rested mama is better for everyone in the home.

> Remember that your sleep is valuable. A well-rested mama is better for everyone in the home.

Creating a routine with some or all of these methods can give your body cues that it's time to relax and sleep now. Turn down the lights, diffuse your essential oil, turn on the white noise, lean back on your pillow, read about your favourite saint, and journal or pray about your day. Then turn off the lights and close your eyes.

While it's tempting to feel like you might as well be productive since you aren't sleeping, I recommend staying in bed. Even when I'm tossing and turning, I often feel like I'm closer to sleep than I would be if I got up to vacuum, wash dishes, or check email. Try to focus on calming actions that will aid sleep in coming rather than giving up on it ever happening.

CHAPTER NINETEEN

Dealing with Your Birthing Emotions

During my first pregnancy, I remember thinking my next pregnancies would be easier because I'd know what to expect. I talked to a lot of friends and read a lot of books, but reading about birth is nothing like actually giving birth. Kind of like reading about Mt. Everest and actually climbing it yourself.

As I faced my third birth, I realized I still didn't know what to expect.

My first two birth experiences were, in many ways, very different.

Sunshine was born on her due date; Lily was born a week late.

Sunshine's labour began as bad backaches every seven minutes; Lily's labour began as mild abdominal cramps every ten or fifteen minutes.

Sunshine's labour began early in the morning and went until late afternoon; Lily's labour began in late afternoon and went until early morning.

I had back labour with Sunshine and front labour with Lily.

I pushed for forty minutes with Sunshine, but five minutes with Lily.

Because we moved so much, I had different care providers for each of my pregnancies. With my third pregnancy, I had a midwife whom I trusted. In fact, at times I was amazed when I said, "No, I don't want _____" and the midwife said, "Okay."

I didn't have to present all my research? Explain why I don't want that test or procedure? Great. That was a huge change from Lily's birth, where I felt like I was in a losing fight and had no control over what happened to me—or to Lily—once I went to the hospital.

And yet… as I faced my third pregnancy, I realized I was scared of the pain. When my second kidney stone hit in my second trimester, and I writhed in pain on my bed, I thought about going into labour. I knew I'd be dealing with a similar pain (though kidney stone pain is worse because it doesn't take a break like contractions) for ten or more hours.

I thought, "I don't want to do that again. I'll take a C-section or an epidural now." I'd hoped that Lily's birth would be faster and easier than Sunshine's, but it wasn't. I didn't want to cling to that hope for my third birth.

Pam England says in *Birthing From Within*, "Who you are in labour and as a mother is merely an extension of who you are in the rest of your life. So if you want to be present and strong in birth, you need to practice that way of being in your everyday life."

I meditated on that quote and what it meant to me. I could see how my birthing choices fit in with my personality and other choices I've made in my life. So how could I live as the woman I wanted to be, not just in giving birth but every day?

Sometimes I wondered if I was making too much out of birth. Why did it matter so much to me where and how I delivered my babies? I didn't find the answer to that, but in reading birth stories online, I saw a common theme: birth *is* a big deal.

A baby's physical entrance into this world is an amazing, emotional, miraculous event. Birth has a profound impact on every woman who goes through it. So I read books about birth by women I respected, such as Pamela England and Ina May Gaskin. I talked to my friends about our birth experiences. I journaled about what I was feeling and asked for intercession from my favourite saints.

And then, I gave birth. A baby's arrival is something that happens, whether we're ready or not. Nine months of preparation can feel both too long and too short. Yet there comes a time when reading another birthing book isn't helpful.

What you need to do is trust your body, your Creator, and your birth team and just push that baby out into this world.

CHAPTER TWENTY

Choosing the Best Car Seat for Your Baby

For new parents, a car seat is one of the biggest and most important purchases to be made before baby's arrival. Since my oldest daughter was born, we've bought several car seats.

Make sure you are getting the right car seat for your baby's size. There are specific safety recommendations for car seats. It's also a good idea to check the manufacturer's requirements to make sure the car seat is best for your baby.

For example, a friend of mine had twins, whom she knew would likely be preemie. That meant she had to find a car seat that would accommodate their small size at first. Not all car seats have straps that adjust to tiny newborns.

Try the car seat in your vehicle before buying it. You can ask a store employee for help in taking the car seat out to your vehicle to make sure it fits. (If the employee won't help you, go to another store.)

When Sunshine was two, we had two vehicles—a Dodge Dakota truck and a Volkswagen Jetta car—and discovered that car seats fit different vehicles. One of our car seats wouldn't fit very well in the narrow back seat of the truck. A friend of mine had a similar problem; she actually upgraded from a small car to a minivan because her car seat was too big for the car.

You'll also want to ask how washable the car seat is. One of our car seats didn't have a removable cover. I learned the hard way, after an incident of motion sickness, how hard it was to clean. When its expiry date finally arrived, I was excited to throw it out.

It's also important to check safety ratings and reviews for the car seat you're considering. Find out what other parents think of the car seat and how easy it is to install, use, and clean. Safety ratings are more important than price. Some budget-friendly car seats have better safety ratings than very expensive models.

Finally, install the car seat properly. Read both your vehicle owner's manual for the proper placement of the car seat in your vehicle and the car seat instruction manual for proper installation. If in doubt, look up car seat safety clinics in your town. They are often offered by your fire hall or local baby store.

Which car seat is best for you?

Most babies start their car rides in an infant bucket seat. We've used an infant bucket seat for all of our babies. While these seats come in a variety of sizes and styles, most have a base which can be left in the vehicle. This makes it easy to get the bucket seat in and out of the vehicle, especially if baby is sleeping.

The advantage of the infant bucket seat is its portability. You can buckle baby into the car seat in the house. If you live in cold climates, you can ensure baby is bundled against the weather before taking her out to the

Check safety ratings and reviews for the car seat you're considering. Find out what other parents think of the car seat and how easy it is to install, use, and clean.

vehicle. If baby falls asleep in the vehicle, you can take baby and bucket into the house to let baby finish his nap.

Many bucket seats are available as part of a travel system. This allows you to take the seat out of the vehicle and snap it onto the stroller. If you are frequently out for errands or kids' activities while the baby naps, this is handy.

If the family has more than one vehicle, or if you are carpooling with another mom, it's easy to transfer the bucket seat between vehicles. If the bucket comes with a snap-in base, you can usually buy a second base for your second vehicle.

The disadvantage of infant bucket seats is their short lifespan. Most babies outgrow their bucket seat around one year. I was able to use our first bucket seat for my first three girls. It then expired and we had to get a new bucket seat for Pearl and Joey. Because car seats cannot be sold secondhand, you'll likely only use the bucket seat during infancy and it will spend a lot of time in storage. I did lend our bucket seat to a friend for her baby between Pearl and Joey.

Convertible car seats can be used for most of a baby's life, from newborn to toddler. These car seats are designed to be installed rear-facing when a baby is young and then turned around when baby is big enough. Convertible car seats offer parents a good deal, as one car seat will likely serve the child until he or she is big enough for a booster seat.

The con to all-in-one car seats is their lack of portability. If baby falls asleep in the car, you might disturb her when getting her out of her car seat. The car seat is also harder to take out and place in another vehicle.

Once our babies outgrew their bucket seats, we switched to convertible car seats. I kept Pearl and Joey rear-facing for a while longer. When rear-facing, they could see their three sisters (sitting in the back of the van). The older girls helped keep the baby entertained in the car. It's also safer to keep babies rear-facing for as long as possible.

For more specific details about the car seats we've used, go to thekoalamom.com and search "car seat review."

CHAPTER TWENTY-ONE

Should You Write a Birth Plan?

Several years after Lily's birth, I flipped through a file I've kept of pregnancy/birth-related information and found the birth plan I wrote. A few things on it surprised me. There were things my doctor had crossed out, refusing to agree to despite the hours I spent researching, reading, and thinking about what went into that birth plan.

Then in the middle of the page was one little line that brought back a flood of memories: "Immediate skin-to-skin contact and nursing after birth."

My memories of Lily's birth are that the nurses were great. One remained in the room with us at all times. She stayed out of the way, quietly observing while I laboured (after she'd asked her long list of intake questions).

The nurses were the ones who caught Lily because the on-call doctor didn't make it to the hospital until after she was born. But one of my clearest memories is the two nurses scrubbing my purple, screaming baby with rough white towels while I begged them, "Let me hold her! Let me hold her!"

In *Birthing From Within*, Pamela England says, "The idea of planning a birth is naive; labor and birth are not events conducive to being planned." As I compared my labours, I saw the truth in her words.

I like being in control; I like planning and knowing what to expect. In Lily's case, because of the shortage of doctors and the hospital policies in our small town, I felt completely out of control. I was stressed and scared that my desires for a natural birth would not be respected.

Pam explains that "the need to write a birth plan invariably comes from: anxiety and/or mistrust of the people who will be attending you, a natural fear of the unknown." It also comes from "Lack of confidence in self and/or [your] birth-partner's ability to express and assert what is needed in the moment."

Check, check, check for the reasons I wrote Lily's birth plan. I didn't write a birth plan for any of my other babies; I simply talked with my midwives about the options available to me. I felt confident that they knew what I wanted and I knew how they could help me.

With my fourth and fifth pregnancies, I continued to read and research birth because I still like to be prepared, but I knew I could trust my midwives and my body to do what needed to be done when baby decided to come.

Pam adds, "There are no unique birth plans. While your birth plan is unique to you, it won't seem that way to your hospital or doctor. All women ask for the same thing: respect, dignity, support to birth naturally with minimal routine intervention and no unnecessary separation from baby."

A friend of mine showed me her birth plan, having also discovered it about the time I was rereading mine. Her daughter often babysat mine, so she'd written her plan about a decade before I wrote mine. I smiled as I saw the similarities between what we wanted. Her birth plan was much more detailed, but we both basically asked for the same thing.

Should you write a birth plan? I think that depends on your personality and situation. Pam's words resonated with me, but at the time of Lily's birth, I had no other options—I couldn't switch care providers. My birth plan was my only way to try to work with my doctor for the birth I wanted. It also allowed me to visualize what I wanted and didn't want in birth.

Pam talks about using birth art and imagination to prepare yourself for the work of labour. I tend to write, rather than draw, so as I explored my concerns and thoughts about birth, it came out in words, such as my birth plan, blog posts, and journal entries.

If that is useful to you or helps you to discuss your birth ideas with your care providers, by all means, do it. If creating your birth plan makes you more fearful about birth, then I recommend other ways of thinking positively about birth.

CHAPTER TWENTY-TWO

Giving Birth Is Better Than You Think

"If pregnancy is this hard, what can labour be like?" a friend of Anna's asked. Here's six reasons birth is better than you think:

1. After all the waiting, the getting bigger, the feeling awkward, the heartburn and poor sleeps, labour sets you free. It is like an awesome thunderstorm relieving the pressure of dense dark clouds … and making way for the sunshine of your child's first smile.

2. Even if you're nervous, you're much stronger than you think. Your body is an amazing participant in the creation of new life, and you'll discover your autopilot knows what to do.

3. Weakness is okay. A delicate flower can open and reveal new life, and gentleness is one of a mother's greatest gifts.

4. Patience, which is love extended over time, will carry you through. Try to offer up each moment for a special prayer intention; it will help the time pass. Ask for whatever help you need, whether it's to hold hands, drink lemonade, be held tight, or be given space. Embrace your labour for what it is, and don't worry too much about how you planned it. Being at peace with how it actually happens is even better.

5. Giving birth is wonderful because, in a way like never before, your husband is going to be completely awed by you, revering your ability to lovingly bring forth a miracle: your baby, the incarnation of your love. You will fall in love again, with your baby, yes, but also with each other.

6. After all the tense waiting and preparation, as before the grand opening of an art show or piano concert, it ends in the revelation of your masterpiece. Applause! You will never see something more beautiful than that tiny newborn face, those little dark eyes looking at you for the first time.

You can do it! And it'll be more worth it than you can imagine.

CHAPTER TWENTY-THREE

New Mamas Need Meals

I was among the first of my friends to get married and have a baby. When I was expecting Sunshine, my college girlfriends threw me a lovely baby shower. I admired the adorable baby blankets, onesies, books, and toys they picked, and packed them neatly away, feeling ready for baby's arrival.

After Sunshine's birth, one of my good friends dropped by to visit. I asked her to hold Sunshine while I switched a load of laundry over. Otherwise, despite my exhaustion, we just chatted.

Recently, she had her first baby. When I called her a few weeks after her baby's birth (to give her time to recover), she said, "Bonnie, I'm sorry. I had no idea what you needed back then!"

I laughed and said, "That's okay. I didn't know what I needed then either." And then I added, "But now I *do* know what *you* need, and I'm too far away to help!" I had sent her a set of Mother Load bags and a toy for her baby, but what I really wanted to do was take a meal to her.

After Sunshine's birth, one couple whom my husband knew offered to drop off a meal for us. They had two kids and a few nights after Sunshine's birth, they came by our apartment with a hot chicken casserole. We invited them in to eat with us, but they refused, saying "congratulations" and leaving. We sat down to eat our meal together, a bit puzzled that they would just leave food and go. Still, it was nice to not cook that night.

When Lily was born, we had moved twice and had no community nearby. My mother-in-law dropped in to help when she could, but otherwise we were on our own with a new baby and a toddler. I remember days of exhaustion as I struggled to balance the needs of my two daughters. Then we packed up our place and moved in with my in-laws for several weeks before moving all the way out to Vancouver Island.

Hours after Jade's birth, my cousin stopped by to say "congratulations" and leave us some baked goods. That night, her sister came over with a casserole dish for us. My brother-in-law and his wife brought a roast chicken and French bread. Other friends showered us with food so that for the first week after Jade's birth, I didn't have to cook. It was amazing.

I understood the gesture my husband's friends had made when Sunshine was born.

The nicest thing for a mom with a new baby is to be mothered a bit!

If your friends ask how they can help you or what they can get you, suggest a meal. Gift cards for restaurants that will deliver or stores that offer ready-made meals are excellent ideas. Your friends could also organize a meal train or meal shower for you.

In a meal train, friends sign up to bring meals on a specific day. Having a meal come every second day often works well, as you can eat leftovers on the other days.

MealTrain.com is an online tool that can help you (or a friend of yours) coordinate meals. There is a place to list favourite meals or let people know about allergies or any other preferences so the food can be the most helpful. You can suggest fruit and veggie trays, muffins, and other snacks as well as meals. MealTrain.com will even send reminder emails to those who've signed up.

Like me, Anna was the very lucky recipient of meal trains since having her second baby. She agrees that it's always such a help. These meals are a special part of making baby's first days smoother and more peaceful.

If you have a freezer, fill it with meals before baby arrives. During my third trimester with Pearl and Joey, I made double batches of whatever I was cooking for supper and then froze half of it. Casseroles and soups are easy to double and freeze.

I also prepped quite a few "freezer meals" that I could simply pull out, dump in the crock pot, and forget about until supper time. For ideas, search "freezer meals" on Pinterest. (If you have older children, this is another way they can help get ready for the baby. My girls had fun chopping vegetables and measuring spices to make our freezer meals. I just had to keep track of who was making what recipe in which Ziploc bag!)

You can also check out what grocery stores are conveniently located to either your home or your husband's place of work. Most grocery stores have ready-to-grab meals like baked chicken, soups and stews, potato salads, bread or buns, etc. Your husband can grab frozen pizzas or chicken nuggets to throw in the oven when he gets home.

Baking is always nice to have around the home after a new baby too. Muffins and quick breads make for great breakfast or snack ideas (especially if you have toddlers or older children who get hangry!). Bread or buns can supplement any meal and make leftovers stretch further.

Labour & Birth

Darling, I'd like to write you beautiful poems
after your long-awaited arrival
and the desperate relief of the moment
you came slipping out like a selkie
from the waters inside
and beached yourself on my belly….
But right now I'm in such a happy bubble
that all I can think is silly mama speak
you little pink piglet sweetie pie flower bud
baby blossom wonderful one
You are warm
You are safe
You are here
You are here
You are here.

~ Anna Eastland

CHAPTER TWENTY-FOUR

How to Prevent Tearing During Labour

Our bodies are wonderful, amazing creations, and nothing proves that more than birthing. I'm constantly amazed at how my body can nourish and grow an entirely new life and then stretch to the extreme in order to allow that new life to enter the world.

And yet—that can also be scary. You may not want to think about the possibility of tearing during labour, but, as with so many other things about birthing, it's better to consider it and be prepared.

During my first pregnancy, tearing was mentioned to me as a possible side effect of labour. The midwives mentioned that they wouldn't perform episiotomies (a rather old-fashioned idea that a woman's body needs to be cut to let the baby out) but otherwise didn't discuss it much. I tore a bit with Sunshine's birth and required a few stitches.

With Lily, I was obsessed with the idea of a "better" birth. I researched quite a bit about tearing and how to prevent it. One idea suggested to me was that birth position could affect how much a woman tore. I decided that I'd push Lily out squatting, rather than lying down. And that's what I did, but I tore worse with Lily than with Sunshine.

Hindsight about both those births let me think about what had worked and what hadn't worked. With my next three pregnancies, I talked with my midwives and, during labour, followed their advice. I didn't tear at all with those pregnancies.

Here's what may help you prevent tearing during labour.

1. Prepare your body.

During your third trimester, start exercises to strengthen your pelvic floor muscles. These are commonly known as Kegels and involve tightening your bum as if you're trying not to poop, holding it for a few seconds, and releasing again. Doing squats can also help stretch and strengthen your pelvic floor muscles.

2. Warm washcloths.

As your baby begins to crown, and you get close to pushing, have your caregiver or birth assistant place a warm washcloth on your bottom. This can help ease the pain, but the warmth may also help your muscles relax and stretch further.

Preparing warm washcloths can be a great task for your husband or doula. Discuss this idea with your care provider and consider how to make it work at your birth place. If you are birthing in a hospital, ask about this on your pre-birth hospital tour. You may need to bring your own cloths.

If you are birthing at home, consider buying a set of cloths to use during birth. You may be able to simply run them in hot water (if there is a sink near where you plan to deliver the baby). Another idea I've seen is to use a crock pot to keep cloths warm.

2. Go slowly.

As you go through transition and into pushing, follow your prenatal care provider's cues. (This may, however, depend upon your care provider. I had more direct support and assistance from my last three midwives than my first two care providers.) I realized the reason I tore so badly with Lily was that I pushed her out very fast.

By the time the urge to push hit me, I was so tired I just wanted labour to be over. The nurses were scrambling to get into the scrubs and telling me not to push yet. My doula tried to tell me to blow instead of pushing. Angry that the nurses weren't ready when I was, and impatient to hold my baby, I ignored their advice and pushed as hard as I could. Lily was born in only a few pushes, but my body paid for it.

With my last three babies, I was more willing to listen to my midwives' advice. When they said wait and go slow, I did that, even when it hurt. A few moments of pain during labour will save you more pain and discomfort later. At one point with Jade, several moments passed with just her head out. It felt terribly uncomfortable ("There's a head in my butt!") but my body needed that time to stretch before I carefully pushed again and let her out.

When you feel the urge to push, focus on your breathing rather than your pushing. Most of us tense and hold our breath to push, which doesn't help either us or baby. The urge to push is actually your uterus contracting to push baby out, so work on breathing to give your uterus the oxygen it needs to do its work.

As you feel the "ring of fire," you may want to push harder to get through it. However, this is your body letting you know that everything is stretching. Think of this as an orange "caution" sign. Slow down and let your body stretch! Keep breathing through the pain and listen to your care provider.

3. Consider your birth position.

I wasn't entirely wrong, during my second pregnancy, with my idea that birth position affected my body's ability to stretch during labour. Studies have shown that birthing standing, squatting or kneeling may help protect your perineum.

Lying down puts more pressure on your bottom. Squatting, standing or kneeling help open your pelvic area and your perineum, giving more space for baby to slide out. However, if you're squatting, avoid spreading your knees too far apart, as this can stretch your perineum sideways. (Perhaps I was doing that with Lily.)

These tips may prevent tearing. Other factors can affect your likelihood to tear, including the size of your baby, your ethnic background, your weight, etc. First-time mothers are also more likely to tear. If you do tear, follow your doctor's instructions to care for yourself. This doesn't indicate a failure on your part, and you will heal!

CHAPTER TWENTY-FIVE

Dealing with Labour Pain

A book about pregnancy wouldn't be complete without a chapter on labour pain. And if you've skipped ahead to this chapter … I'm not going to promise you a scream-free birth. I did birth all five of my babies without pain medication. It does hurt, but the pain *is* worth it when you're holding your new little baby. Here's what has helped me get through labour.

1. Know yourself.

As you head into labour, think very deeply about yourself and how you deal with pain. What's the hardest thing you have ever done in your life? What's the most painful thing you've endured? What helped you get through that?

One thing I reflected on was an overnight hike I'd done with my mom about halfway through university. We were excited to get out for the May long weekend, but snowy weather forced us to change our plans. We ended up hiking forty kilometers in two days—after I'd basically done little but carry my books from one classroom to another for two years. I hurt. The last eight kilometers of that hike were intense, but I kept putting one foot in front of the other and I made it.

That hike happened a few years before I prepared to give birth to Sunshine. As I thought about the hike, I saw a few similarities between it and the labour I'd soon face.

First, I am strong. There may be moments in labour when you think you can't do it. When you want to quit or give up. That's when your support team can remind you that you can do this, but you also need to reach deep within yourself to find your own strength to keep going.

If you have a moment like that in the past, where you pushed through the pain and did something you thought you couldn't do, reflect on that moment as you prepare for and go into labour.

Second, I knew I didn't want my mom with me at the hospital. My mom is awesome and we are very similar, but she is very chipper and positive and that totally grated on me when I just wanted to curl up in a ball under my pack at the side of the trail.

Pain affects each of us in different ways. I tend to pull into myself, stop talking, and just focus on getting through it. Knowing that, I choose to have only my husband with me at the hospital (besides my care providers).

If, on the other hand, you find your mom or sister or another person comforting to have nearby when you are in pain, invite them to support you at your birth (if possible).

2. Know your reasons.

I won't tell you that you should have a natural birth just because I did. If you choose to have an epidural or laughing gas, I won't judge you. I will encourage you to do your research about labour, think about what you need, and talk to your husband and care provider about what's best for you and your baby.

I had normal, problem-free pregnancies, encouraging friends, and deeply held reasons for wanting a natural birth. Even when I was deep in pain and wanted to beg for that epidural, I knew *why* I had made this choice. That *why* helped me keep going.

Your support team can remind you that you can do this, but you also need to reach deep within yourself to find your own strength to keep going.

Friends of mine have had epidurals and C-sections and other birth interventions. Sometimes these are necessary and helpful. Every woman and every pregnancy are different. Pain is tough, so if you are going to endure it, know why you are doing it. Why do you want or not want an epidural? Make sure your husband or care providers knows this too so that they can support you in labour (and remind you about your why if necessary). You should also discuss with your care provider when a change of plans may be necessary. For example, even if you know you don't want an epidural, when might it be required?

3. Try a TENS.

TENS stands for "transcutaneous electrical nerve stimulation" and is a drug-free method of managing pain during labour. During my third labour, I borrowed a TENS unit from my midwife. Your care provider might also be able to loan you a TENS or you can buy them online.

A TENS is a small, handheld unit that has several electrodes which you attach to your body using small pads. You then press a button on the TENS to send mild electrical pulses through your skin to your spinal cord and brain. These pulses can help lower your pain or distract you from it.

The TENS can be stopped or started at any time. For example, I used it in early labour with Jade, took it off to get in the shower, and then put it back on again later. Towards transition, it stopped helping with my pain, so I took it off and used other methods for getting through each contraction.

A variety of studies have been done with TENS units to see if they help with labour pain. It does seem to reduce labour pain, and most women who used it said they would use it again, but the studies are somewhat inconclusive.

One of the advantages to the TENS is that the woman in labour is in control of it. This sense of control (or being able to do something about your pain) might be part of what helps.

4. Touch and massage.

Massage, hand-holding, hair brushing and other gentle touches may help distract you from labour pain. (Or you may find it annoying and too distracting at certain stages of labour. This goes back, a bit, to knowing yourself and what you like and communicating that to your support team, both before and during labour.)

Touch is something your doula or husband can help you with during labour. Massage during labour may work best if your husband has some practice with this beforehand. (If labour is the first time he's ever given you a massage, it may not be as comforting or distracting!) Try some massages before you go into labour to see what works and what you appreciate. Using coconut or almond oil while massaging may make it feel better.

The doula I hired for Lily's birth suggested I bring my hairbrush with me. I love having someone play with my hair, so I followed her suggestion. Before transition, she spent quite a bit of time brushing my hair. Make sure to communicate with your support person about what is working. Do you want your hair brushed during or between contractions?

Your doula or husband may also simply provide a hand to hold. With Lily, my husband stood behind me, arms wrapped around me, supporting me during contractions. His warmth and strength helped me get through quite a few contractions. This was another idea from my doula; if you aren't hiring a doula, look up ideas in books like *Husband-Coached Childbirth.*

5. Mentally refocus.

Pain gets worse when we focus on it, yet our brains can also be easy to distract. Touch, TENS, and intellectual reasons help take your attention off the pain of labour and onto something else. You can also bring other things with you to labour to help you refocus mentally.

For example, during Sunshine's birth, I brought a small photo album with some of my favourite photos. I flipped through this myself or had my husband hold it for me. When a contraction hits, pick a picture to focus on and concentrate on putting yourself in that moment—maybe a moment from your honeymoon, or wedding, or dating days, or childhood. Pick strong, happy memories that will be easy to step into in your imagination.

Music is another good distraction. Make a playlist of songs that inspire or encourage you. Videos of women dancing through labour have gone viral on Facebook. Music does encourage us to move and to have a positive attitude, and that can help greatly when you're in labour. Staying active during labour lets gravity pull the baby down as well as reduce your pain.

I've turned to prayer and meditation on Scripture or the lives of the saints during labour. Jesus came to Earth as a tiny baby, so I ask Him to pray for my own baby as he or she enters the world. His mother Mary knows what it's like to endure childbirth (under adverse circumstances!), so I ask her to pray for me.

Other saints who were moms or endured terrible pain for the sake of the Gospel help me to see the good (my baby!) that will come from this pain. When pain has a purpose, it's easier to endure.

6. Move it.

Stay upright and active for as long as you can during labour. With Lily, I walked the hospital hallways in early labour. With Jade, I walked my neighbourhood and then went up and down my stairs. Again, movement helps you think about something other than your pain and also helps your body move the baby out.

With Sunshine, I used an exercise ball. The birthing centre had these available for use by moms, but if yours does not, you may be able to bring your own. Rocking back and forth on the ball helped ease the pain in my back during labour.

For my last three babies, I did squats beside the bed. This wasn't something I remember coming across in all my research or reading before birth. It was simply something I did instinctively during Jade's labour that I found helpful. I'd curl up on my bed between contractions and then when a contraction hit, I'd stand up and go into squats. The midwives were amazed at me, but it helped!

Knowing that had helped with Jade, I also did it with Pearl and Joey. Squats are good because they open your pelvic floor area.

7. Smell it.

Scents have strong memories and associations for most of us. The smell of oranges always takes me back to Christmas mornings in my childhood (no matter how many mandarins I've eaten!). Scents can help you during labour too. My doula brought oranges to Lily's birth and peeled them for me to hold when nausea hit. That strong, fresh citrus smell took my mind off the pain and staved off my nausea for a bit.

Essential oils may also be helpful (although these may be easier to use if you're having a homebirth). I prepared a few essential oil rollers before Joey's birth and had them with the rest of my birthing stuff. Several times, I rubbed oils across my belly to help with the pain. My midwives were okay with this. My husband doesn't like strong scents but put up with it for me.

8. Warm water.

In all my labours, I've spent some time in either the shower or the bath. The birthing centre where Sunshine was born had both a huge shower and a huge tub, and I moved back and forth between the two. For my other labours, I've just used the shower.

Warm water helps relax muscles and also eases pain. I've often climbed into a warm bath when I'm not pregnant to ease a backache. It also works for back labour pain! If the shower head is adjustable, then you can point it directly at your back or stomach (or have your husband hold it for you).

For a couple of my pregnancies, I wore a bikini or tankini during labour. This let me get in and out of the tub or shower and also gave me some modesty around my midwives. It's easy to put on a robe or wrap up in a towel or blanket when you step out of the water.

Anna has had water births for most of her babies and recommends it. If your hospital or birthing centre offers the option, talk to your care provider about it. Water births may also help prevent tearing as the baby is born.

If a shower or tub isn't an option, use a hot water bottle instead. Your husband or doula can keep a couple hot water bottles full and hot and place them against your back or abdomen as the pain comes and goes.

I hope these tips help! If you hire a doula, or have a midwife, they may also have other suggestions or recommendations for you to consider.

CHAPTER TWENTY-SIX

My Favourite Things to Bring to the Hospital

1. My husband. His job is to stay close, pass me lemonade and then look adorable holding our newborn.
2. My own cozy quilt, because it's warmer and more comforting than thin hospital blankets, especially after a water birth, which I usually have. I love the giant birthing tubs at the hospital; it's like being held in a giant warm embrace while giving birth.
3. My favourite take-out food, so I can have a solid meal as soon as I want after birth.
4. Plenty of snacks, such as trail mix and granola bars, and lemonade.
5. A beloved childhood novel to reread, such as *Little Women* or *Anne of Green Gables*, because it's comforting to take those familiar people with me and to enjoy while I'm resting and nursing the baby. With a large family at home, staying a few days at the hospital with only one baby is like a mini vacation!
6. Heavy duty pads in my purse for after birth, even though the hospital provides them too.
7. A change of comfy clothes, pajamas, and slippers.
8. An overnight bag for my husband, too, who will likely end up sleeping in the hospital room with me. A clean shirt, socks, underwear, deodorant, toothbrush, brush, etc. And a book for him, too.
9. A few little, tiny outfits for new baby and some swaddling blankets.
10. A few newborn diapers with the soft curved top to go under the umbilical cord clamp.

11. A newborn bucket car seat—can't leave the hospital without it!

12. A lot of hope and the strength of knowing many friends are praying for a safe labour for me. I have a bunch of friends I text or email when I'm heading to the hospital who cheer me on from afar.

13. My iPad mini to take pictures and send them to my loved ones when baby arrives.

14. My midwife. Actually, several times my midwife brought me to the hospital because we don't have a car! I can't express enough the great privilege of having midwives journey through pregnancy with me, becoming my friends and supporting me in this epic event of giving birth. It means a lot to be supported by women I feel at home with during labour.

With all the amenities of the hospital, and the personal care of my midwives, I know I'm in good hands.

CHAPTER TWENTY-SEVEN

How to Make Padsicles

One thing I've found to greatly help my healing postpartum is padsicles. These are giant sanitary pads with witch hazel, aloe, and essential oils put in the freezer to get cold and then placed in your underwear to soothe your sore bottom.

Start with natural pads. My first midwives recommended avoiding most brand-name pads, which contain chemicals and perfumes that could prevent healing. Natural pads can be hard to find (try natural health stores or online wellness stores) and may not come in sizes quite as big as brand-name pads, but they are worth it. With my second daughter, I lived in a small town and couldn't find natural pads readily, so I used brand-name pads. I did notice that healing took longer than previous or later births.

Unwrap your pads carefully, keeping the wrapper. I like to make about five padsicles at a time, but you could make more, depending on freezer space and how many pads you need in your first few days postpartum.

Pour a few tablespoons of witch hazel onto the pad. Witch hazel contains tannins that can help reduce swelling, repair broken skin, and fight bacteria—all useful properties for your post-birth lady parts.

Squirt some aloe gel onto the pad. Aloe is antibacterial and helps heal cuts and tears.

Be careful about buying aloe gel, as many brands contain extra preservatives, colouring, and other chemicals that are not helpful. Aloe is naturally clear, so avoid any aloe products that are bright green. JASON has a great gel that is 98 percent aloe, completely natural, and has worked well for me for padsicles and other uses.

Add a few drops of lavender essential oil. Lavender is regenerative, antibacterial, and can act as a mild pain reliever too. It also has a pleasant, calming scent.

Carefully fold your pads and wrap them up again, then place them in a plastic bag in your freezer. Allow them to freeze for a few hours. I usually prepare several of these before baby is born to have ready immediately after birth.

The pads are pretty cold when you first put them on, but the chill subsides in a few seconds and then the cold feels good. The witch hazel, aloe, and lavender will improve healing and ease pain. You can switch to smaller pads when your bleeding subsides or stop using them when you feel good. I don't usually wear padsicles past my first week postpartum, but listen to your body and what is working for you.

CHAPTER TWENTY-EIGHT

Easy, Natural Ways to Get Labour Going

Having given birth eight times, and most of those times several weeks early on purpose, I (Anna) have a lot of experience with using natural methods of getting labour going. Why?

During all but one of my pregnancies, I had a liver condition called cholestasis, which makes the body not process toxins properly. Instead, it hangs on to them and deposits them under the skin. The first sign of it is usually feeling itchy on your hands and the soles of your feet. Then if it's getting worse, your urine darkens and you get super itchy everywhere. There is medicine you can take to help with this condition, so make sure to consult your caregiver if you begin to have itchy hands and feet and wonder if you might have cholestasis. A simple blood test can tell you.

Cholestasis is increasingly dangerous for the baby as pregnancy progresses, as the body can no longer keep your insides clean. The baby needs to be born as soon as he is "no longer squishy in the middle," so usually at 37 or 38 weeks. I have been able, with the help of my midwives, to deliver this early each time using noninvasive, natural methods, such as those listed below. This has meant I haven't been forced to resort to more intense chemical methods such as an oxytocin drip, which can make contractions not only stronger but more painful. So in consultation with your care provider, I highly recommend trying our tips to help get labour going whether you need to deliver early, on time, or are already late.

Tips for Encouraging Labour

Watch a funny movie with your husband (laughter is good for you both!).

Wash the floor on your hands and knees. The position and motion will help baby move towards the birth canal, and you'll feel better about nice floors.

Order in (or make) your favourite spicy foods! Mexican or East Indian are great options.

Do squats! These open up your pelvic floor area and stretch your muscles. To help myself remember, I try to do ten of them each time I go to the washroom within a week of my hoped-for delivery date.

Turn on a workout or dance video and get moving! You can do this with your older kids or husband for more fun. Shake that baby out!

Ask hubby for some hugs and snuggles. Friendly touches release oxytocin and help get things going. If you feel up for some lovemaking too, that can also help.

Get a pedicure or ask hubby or a friend for a really good foot massage. Your feet are usually sore from supporting your extra weight anyway, and it's hard to trim or paint your own toenails. Strong pressure in the centre of the tender area of your heel can help induce labour.

Ask your friends or mom's group to pray for you. We both appreciate having this spiritual and emotional support during this time.

The Labour Cocktail

We recommend consulting your care provider before taking this labour cocktail. Your midwife may have her own labour cocktail recipe or recommendations for you. A doctor may be less supportive but should still be aware that you are planning to encourage labour to begin.

Castor oil on its own is hard on your stomach. Taking it in this cocktail helps prevent diarrhea or other side effects. Castor oil can cause a slightly higher chance of meconium (it affects baby the same way it affects you).

The labour cocktail shouldn't be tried before your due date (unless you have a medical reason like Anna's). Do try to follow the above tips as well to help your body prepare for labour.

Anna's labour cocktail recipe:

2 tbsp. castor oil

Thick juice such as apricot or mango

¼ cup almond or nut butter

Mix all together in a blender. Try to drink fairly quickly—within half an hour or so, but know it's a bit intense (okay, gross sludge), so it might take you longer.

Reduce Your Stress

I (Bonnie) have had slightly different experiences with my pregnancies. My first was born on her due date.

My second was born a week late amidst much stress. My doctor mentioned induction even before I'd hit my due date. I looked up castor oil to encourage baby to come before induction was necessary but read enough warnings about it online that I didn't try it.

My third was born two weeks late, but my midwives were willing to give me time to wait. Finally, they recommended a labour cocktail (similar to Anna's) with castor oil and verbena oil. They gave me the recipe and told me when and how to take it.

My fourth was expected to be late due to my previous history. Instead, thanks to prayer and my diet of dates, red raspberry leaf tea, and evening primrose oil, she was born on her due date.

My fifth was born just a few days after his due date, but his arrival was perfect. My midwives were swamped on the weekend of his due date, and my mom hadn't arrived to help yet. I wanted him to come after she arrived, so I was preparing a spicy meal for myself and getting ready to make Anna's labour cocktail when I went into labour naturally right after picking Mom up at the airport.

In looking back at my babies who were born "overdue," I can see that stress affected my pregnancy. With my second, I didn't like my doctor/hospital situation (you can read the full story in the birth stories at the end of the book). With my third, my in-laws had arrived to help, but I was worried about how to be a hostess while having a baby. I was excited to have them visiting, but I didn't want to be in labour with them in the house.

With my fourth and fifth, I made sure I was completely ready for baby (including setting up the cradle my husband complained we wouldn't use because our babies always co-slept for the first several months). I worked at dealing with my stress, praying, preparing as best as I could, and letting go of what I couldn't control.

If there are stressful situations surrounding your baby's birth, I encourage you to talk it over with your spouse, care provider, and anyone else who can help. What can you do to reduce your stress and relax to welcome your baby into the world? We react very physically to stress and that can affect labour.

Anna and I have tried to share our advice and experience with you through these pages. We hope this has helped you feel less stressed and more prepared about pregnancy and giving birth.

Fourth Trimester

Just when lights go out
you open your eyes
and decide it's time
for a midnight stroll.

We saunter about the kitchen
as you stare out from the blanket bundle
with your little wise old elf face.

You wrinkle your tiny forehead
and furrow your almost invisible eyebrows,
looking about quizzically
as you ponder some deep truth
until the rapid flutter of your tongue
through pursed lips reveals your babyness
phantom nursing…

You were just spacing out
and daydreaming of milk after all.

~ Anna Eastland

CHAPTER TWENTY-NINE

Dispelling the Myth of Sibling Jealousy

When you go to the library looking for nice kids' books on welcoming a new baby into the family, you are confronted by a disturbing majority of books that focus on sibling jealousy.

They are filled with stories of angry older siblings attempting to put the new babies in a box and ship them back to where they came from. The baby is initially perceived as a noisy, stinky usurper of mom and dad's attention and only accepted near the end of the book as a positive addition to the family.

As a mother of eight, I have not encountered this negative response of older siblings. In fact, I've seen quite the opposite. My kids are excited when I announce a new pregnancy, and my belly receives affectionate hugs and kisses long before baby is showing.

Everyone likes to suggest names and imagine what the baby will look like. They enjoy feeling the baby kick, playing a kind of peekaboo through my belly. The kids are vying for the first turn to hold the baby before I even leave for the hospital.

When I brought our baby son home from the hospital, these are the kind of things the older kids said:

"Oh, he's so cute! He's the cutest baby ever!"
"He's my best friend!"
"I want him to sleep in my bed. I wish I was his mommy."
"Mummy, he made a sad face in his sleep. Is he having a bad dream? He's too little to know it's not real. I wish I could have all the bad dreams so he could have only good dreams."
"Can I hold him? I'll be careful!"
"Our baby is better than presents. He's better than treats. I'd rather stay with him than watch a show."

You get the idea. Each one of my kids, from ages nine to two, responds with smiles, gentle hands and great joy. Having a new baby is a shared experience that brings everyone closer.

The big girls like to help set the table, make breakfast, and amuse the younger ones so I can rest. The little ones have fun playing guard outside my bedroom door: "You're the queen and he's the baby prince. We will guard the door and keep you safe."

From my personal experience, babies are welcomed by little children with love and joy rather than jealousy and suspicion. I think this latter attitude is a projection of parents who feel an unnecessary guilt about bringing a new baby home, as if exclusive parental attention was really the best thing for their older child.

When an older sibling is "dethroned," they have the chance to grow in love and generosity. They learn to care for another more vulnerable than themselves. They also realize the world does not revolve exclusively around their whims and desires. This is a huge life lesson, and one better learned sooner than later.

More children give more opportunities to love. And ultimately parenting is all about teaching our children to love. To care for others. To find joy in self-giving.

When you allow your kids to help you and the new baby in little ways, like fetching a new diaper or burp cloth, or holding the newborn's hands while they have a diaper change, they feel important because they are able to do good. And this is something that makes us all happy, much more than having all the attention and toys to ourselves!

So ignore those silly books and rest in the fact that a new baby is the best gift you can give your child to make them feel secure in the ongoing love of their parents and in the growth of their little world at home, a safe place where they are surrounded by people who love them and whom they love in return.

CHAPTER THIRTY

Breastfeeding Basics

One of the amazing abilities our bodies have, besides growing a baby inside our wombs, is nourishing these little ones after they emerge. In addition to its many nutritional benefits for baby, breastfeeding is a beautiful way for mother and child to bond.

The skin-to-skin contact helps baby adjust to the outside world, making her feel safe and close to mama's familiar heartbeat. It is so adorable to see a newborn snuggling into mama's chest and sucking away with great concentration on his tiny face. Sometimes babies even fall sleep nursing and smile in their sleep— so cute!

But how does this all work? Do babies know how to nurse, or must they be taught? What about moms? Happily, the nurses or midwives attending your birth will help you and baby

One of the amazing abilities our bodies have, besides growing a baby inside our wombs, is nourishing these little ones after they emerge.

get settled in and figure things out. They can show you good ways to hold your baby, gently supporting her neck, while ensuring she's getting a good latch on your nipple, which should be mostly inside her mouth rather than being sucked on like a straw. Baby's jaw muscles develop while nursing as their movement stimulates milk flow.

Nursing also releases the hormone oxytocin, while helps your uterus to contract again after birth, shrinking to its normal tennis ball size. Mom and baby help each other.

These post-labour contractions can be painful though, so don't try to be a hero. Take your pain medication every four hours or so, as indicated, to help your body heal and reduce inflammation. You'll need all your energy to focus on your new baby, and taking care of yourself first enables you to do a better job.

Along those lines, make sure to eat and drink a lot to replenish the energy you spent in labour. You may not have eaten for many hours and may have even thrown up as labour intensified. It can help to have warm tea with milk and honey to restore your blood sugar after birth, followed by a big hot meal!

Nursing takes a lot of calories, so bring snacks to the hospital or order in pizza if you've missed meal-time. (You don't have to eat those cold, unidentifiable hospital meals!) For my last birth, I even brought my favourite East Indian take-out food along. After labour, I had my baby in my arms, my favourite food, and some strong meds to deal with the after-cramps. It was great; only took me eight births to get it right!

While eating well is important for nursing, just as in pregnancy, don't get too stressed out if you're not finding time to make big salads with a newborn. I remember after my first baby was a few weeks old, she was gaining weight well even though babies usually lose some weight after birth.

"What are you eating to make this good milk?" asked my midwife on a home visit.

"Uh, grilled cheese!" I laughed.

Having said that, make sure to say yes any time someone offers to bring a meal! That's their ticket to see baby!

Nursing works on a supply and demand system, so the more your baby nurses, the more milk your breasts will be stimulated to make. For the first few days, it won't seem like much as baby can be quite sleepy, and only requires small amounts.

This first milk is a nutrient-dense substance called colostrum, which is important for baby's transition from umbilical cord feeding to nursing. Usually after a few days, your newborn will perk up and cluster feed, nursing very often, and possibly keeping you up all night!

This might feel crazy, but it's actually a healthy sign: your baby is bringing the milk in—letting your body know what he needs to be healthy and grow. The next day you might be a little shocked at the size of your chest—whoa, mama!

Engorgement can be painful but should only last a few days. Hot showers can help with the pain, and you may even be able to express some breastmilk by hand during your shower. Cabbage leaves are recommended to help as they are cool and curved like your breasts. Simply tuck one into your bra and then remove it when its warm and limp.

If you have a breast pump, a little pumping may help to reduce the pain of engorgement. Avoid pumping too much, however, as that can make your body produce more milk (and worsen the problem). Simply pump a small amount to ease the pain and wait for your body to adjust to baby's needs.

Don't be surprised if you're really emotional around day three after birth. The initial adrenalin from the birth has worn off, and exhaustion is setting in. It's okay to cry, feel overwhelmed and to ask your husband to hold the baby so you can take a shower or nap.

Your baby will likely settle into a routine of eating about every three hours, so you should have a little time between feeds. Growth spurts will be accompanied by cluster feeding, so be attentive to your baby's cues.

Some women have trouble with getting their babies to latch properly and find nursing painful. There is a slight stinging feeling inside your breasts called "let down" when the milk is coming, but it shouldn't hurt much or last very long

> Don't be surprised if you're really emotional around day three after birth... the initial adrenalin from the birth has worn off, and exhaustion is setting in.

If your nipples are getting sore, ask a girlfriend who is more experienced in nursing to give you a hand or talk to your midwives, nurses, or a lactation consultant. There is also a great organization called La Leche League which holds regular meetings for moms and their babies to come discuss nursing and get help.

Some care providers may push you towards bottle feeding, or at least supplementing your breastmilk with formula, but using bottles can cause nipple confusion. Baby may be more prone to drink from the easy-flowing bottle, rather than your breast, which takes more work. Nursing is important for facial muscle development as well as nourishment.

Remember also that because nursing is supply and demand, giving the baby other milk will mean less nursing and therefore less milk and could aggravate the problem.

Give yourself time to get confident. Try to have lots of quiet, skin-to-skin cuddles with your baby. Look for your baby's hunger cues, such as fussing and rooting for the breast by opening her mouth and sucking on anything near—even your chin!

Experiment with different nursing positions and use a nursing pillow if it helps you hold baby close rather than hunching over and hurting your back. Breastfeeding is a unique gift. It helps you slow down and savour time with your baby, and it gives amazing health benefits like boosting your child's immune system.

Truly, the newborn stage will go so fast. Enjoy the rest, for soon enough you'll be chasing around a toddler and hardly sitting down!

You'll likely feel self-conscious about nursing for the first few months. Our culture is growing more comfortable with women breastfeeding in public, but there are still stories of moms who have been shamed. Many churches, malls, and other areas now have nursing mothers rooms where you can feed and change a baby in privacy and comfort.

It is possible to nurse discreetly anywhere, but you may find a nursing cover helpful at first. Others find the nursing cover a hindrance, as it's hard to see baby while feeding. Practice at home to see what works best for you. Layering your clothing or wearing a scarf or sweater can also provide more cover while nursing.

Don't forget to burp your baby after nursing, by putting her up with her head on your shoulder (on a burp cloth or little blanket, if you like) and gently patting her back. This will hopefully prevent painful gas bubbles, which could otherwise wake your infant and rob you of some extra sleep.

If your baby has a gassy tummy, you can also lay her on her back and rotate her legs like a little bicycle in the air or lay her over your knees and gently massage her back with circular movements. You'll discover what works best for you.

Also, be sure to check for issues other than hunger when baby fusses. She could have a dirty diaper, be too hot or cold, or simply want to be walked around the room or cuddled close.

I tended to feed my first daughter any time she fussed at all, and sometimes it was too often. Her little tummy was full to the brim, and I was shocked to see how far she could spit up (yup, projectile vomit) when she had had too much. Live and learn!

Happily, babies live in the moment and are very forgiving as their parents bumble along trying to do so.

CHAPTER THIRTY-ONE

How to Prevent and Treat Mastitis

One of the greatest challenges as a new mom is learning to not just take care of your baby, which is hard enough, but to still take care of yourself. Flooded with feelings of wonder and affection for your new child and exhausted from frequent night wakings, it can be hard to even remember you exist except as your baby's source of milk and comfort.

In the midst of all this, you may feel pressure, whether from others or even yourself, to "get back to normal" or "be productive." Nature has wisely built in some mechanisms to help mothers know when they are overdoing it and to remind them to slow down and take care of themselves. One of them is mastitis.

Mastitis gives a painful bruised feeling in one breast due to a blocked milk duct getting inflamed. The affected area will appear slightly red and be hard or lumpy to the touch. If this doesn't sound too bad, imagine being punched in the chest and also having flu-like symptoms of exhaustion, soreness, and fever.

In my experience, a prime recipe for getting mastitis is spending the whole day out and about visiting or shopping—letting baby sleep too much in her car seat or carrier so she doesn't nurse frequently enough or long enough. Chances are you are also wearing a tight bra instead of your comfy T-shirt or pajamas at home.

Your breasts can become swollen or engorged with too much milk, and a milk duct can get blocked. As your body fights this problem, you begin to feel as if you have the flu. Listen to your body and hurry home to rest and nurse calmly.

To help prevent mastitis, make sure you buy bras or nursing tank tops that fit your new shape properly. Chances are you are much better endowed than before giving birth! Don't cheap out and squeeze into your old bras or tight shirts; instead, enjoy this shopping opportunity and buy what feels right for you now.

Also, nurse your sleepy little newborn often, usually every three hours or so, at least in the daytime. Be careful about spending the whole day out and letting your little one sleep through and skip feeds.

Put you and your baby first and practice saying no to relatives and friends who push you to overdo it in the first few months. They likely mean no harm but simply don't know what you're going through. Trust yourself. Learning to set boundaries is a hugely important life lesson motherhood helps us learn.

Despite your best efforts to prevent it, mastitis can happen, and if left unchecked can lead to high fever and the need for antibiotics. What are some home treatments that can prevent it from getting so bad?

1. Rest.

This is key. You need to give your body a chance to catch up on sleep and rest. So ignore the laundry, order in dinner, and nap with your baby. You're not being lazy—you're preventing a trip to the doctor or hospital.

2. Breastfeed lots.

You may not want anyone coming near your breast when it hurts so much, but not nursing baby would make it worse. Breastfeed often and at length, especially on the affected side, to help unblock the milk duct and drain the milk fully.

3. Warmth.

Heat will help unblock the duct, so take hot showers, lay warm towels on your chest, or sleep cuddling a hot water bottle. Pile on the blankets and sweat it out. See it as a chance to lose some extra fluids you've been retaining since pregnancy.

4. Gentle massage.

Although it's painful, gentle massage in circular motions, from the outside of the breast towards the nipple, can help get milk flowing properly again. You can even gently hand express breastmilk in the hot shower if you're engorged.

5. Play nurse.

Treat yourself the way you'd treat your best friend if she had the flu. Rest, hot fluids like tea and soup, warmth, vitamin C, and garlic will all help. Go gently.

In a few days you should be all better. I've always been able to treat my mastitis this way, over a dozen years of nursing, without having to resort to antibiotics.

Of course, keep an eye on your temperature. If you feel things aren't improving, get in touch with your doctor or midwife for additional help.

CHAPTER THIRTY-TWO

No More Mommy Wars

A hum of conversation filled the room as women nibbled at cheese and fruit and sipped tea while keeping a close eye on nearly a dozen babies attempting to walk or crawl or sit. Around the edges of the room sat a row of blue chairs, each with a white sign balanced on it.

On the walls were photos of various women holding those signs— two or three women in each photo, smiling and leaning together, clearly friends even though the signs they held said opposite things.

I had a homebirth after Caesarean.
I had a hospital birth.
I had a water birth at home.

I use a stroller.
I wear my child.

I work outside the home.
I'm a stay-at-home mom.
I work at home.

No More Mommy Wars!: a photo project was started by mom and blogger Shauna Stewart Douglas. As a new mom, she quickly encountered the judgment that almost every mom today has faced. *You're doing that wrong. You should be doing this. You aren't doing enough.*

Shauna founded a Facebook group for moms in Victoria, BC, to have a safe place to ask questions and share their ideas. Inspired by CT Working Mom's Campaign for Judgement-Free Motherhood, Shauna started her own photo project.

I was thrilled to meet Shauna at a local event and to chat with some other moms as we watched our children play. I also wanted to take my own picture, but I wanted to hold two signs.

My mantra as a mom has been that every family does what is right for their family, and that will look different for each family—and even for each child. My parenting has changed as my children have grown. I picked two signs because I do co-sleep—but I also use a crib. I wear my child, but I have four strollers too.

As I drove to the event, I thought about all the silly things that divide parents and how my own parenting has changed. Before Sunshine was born, a friend of ours shared her enthusiasm for co-sleeping and I listened dubiously, intent on using a crib still—until Sunshine refused to sleep in that crib.

I exclusively cloth-diapered Sunshine, but with my last three babies, I used disposables at night and cloth during the day.

I bought a changing table for Sunshine, like most moms do, but after Jade, I didn't have one, as another friend of ours suggested when Sunshine was little.

As moms and dads, we are all unique. We each have different parenting situations and unique children. And each of us has to figure out how to raise our children in the best way possible. That's not going to look the same for each of us, but we'll find a way that works.

I've had friends ask me how I managed to juggle being a full-time student while having three daughters, but I'm also amazed by the things they accomplish.

As you embark on your own parenting journey, you'll encounter judgment about the choices you make. I wish it wasn't so, but unfortunately, you'll likely need to develop a thick skin. Your friends will accept and support your parenting choices, even if those choices are different than their own choices. If a friend or family member doesn't approve of your parenting style, you may have to set some boundaries for a time.

Read books. Talk with your mom friends. Discuss your ideas with your husband. And then do what feels right for you and your baby at this time. That might change with your next baby or even with baby's next birthday. That's okay.

You're the mom, and you know what's best for your child. Hang onto that (and don't be the one passing on the judgment!).

CHAPTER THIRTY-THREE

"Femachoism"
and the Need for Mom Buddies

A friend and I chatted about motherhood and vulnerability and how tough it is to get some women to open up about how they're really doing after having a new baby. There seems to be, especially among women who are hoping to have multiple children, a feeling that they need to pretend it's easy.

"Of course it's great! Otherwise, why would I do this again? I don't look crazy… do I?"

These kind of sentiments shove any postpartum struggles way down, out of sight.

Sometimes, in the hopes of attracting others to motherhood, moms put on a brave face and only present the good. This is a bit like trying to recruit future Olympic athletes by pretending it's a cake-walk. It's not effective because it's not authentic.

It is better to admit the difficulty and affirm its worth. As G.K. Chesterton insisted, a mother's task is challenging not because it is minute or unimportant but because it is gigantic.

Where do we get this pressure to pretend that one of the most physically and emotionally challenging life experiences—new parenthood—is a smooth ride? It is part of what I like to call "femachosim"—the tendency to be competitive about motherhood and to shy away from admitting any vulnerability or suffering that would seem to indicate weakness.

There is an underlying insecurity in this attitude—a fear of being told suffering is your fault and you shouldn't have wasted time having kids. These things do get said.

In an essay in *Love Rebel: Reclaiming Motherhood*, I discuss this devaluation of motherhood and femininity in general. I question the validity of a feminism that looks down on the intrinsically feminine power of bearing and nurturing children and only values professions that have typically been done by men.

A friend of mine who returned from maternity leave heard comments at her workplace like, "Being a stay-at-home mom is for lazy, lost losers." This attitude can make new moms feel parenting should at least be an easy ride and not a challenge. "How hard can it be? It's just changing diapers, right?" So they hide their struggles.

The fact is that motherhood is extremely hard, besides being beautiful and rewarding, but we moms choose it anyway. We choose the sleepless nights, the intensity of labour, the vulnerability of having our hearts walk around outside of ourselves in tiny little bodies we are totally responsible for. It's overwhelming and exhausting and challenges every fibre of our being.

And we choose it anyway. We choose to love. We choose to give of ourselves constantly. We choose to have enough hope in our world to believe that life is worth living and worth sharing. We don't choose it because it's comfortable. We choose it because it's transformative.

If that's lazy then I need a new dictionary, because I can't imagine how those things are at all connected.

So new moms out there, if you're struggling, reach out. Don't suffer alone and isolate yourself for fear of not being a super-mom.

> Motherhood is extremely hard, besides being beautiful and rewarding, but we moms choose it anyway.

I saw a great T-shirt that said "World's Okayest Mom." It made me laugh so hard! None of us are perfect. But we're in this together, and it's a lot more fun that way.

Spend time with other moms. "Waste" time visiting over coffee. The laughter and conversation you have there can save you hundreds at a therapist later!

Many people suffer from postpartum depression for a time after birthing, and there is help. A good place to start is postpartum.org, which also has great materials for your spouse to read. Your hormones are raging and sleep is a distant dream, so don't beat yourself up if that takes a toll.

Reach out. Talk to your doctor. Talk to friends who are supportive. Take steps to get help. And don't be afraid to ask for it. Lean on others, so they can one day lean on you. That's what friendship is. It enriches life so deeply.

Lean on others, so they can one day lean on you. That's what friendship is. It enriches life so deeply.

With a support network of mom buddies, your life with kids is really awesome despite the difficulties. There are so many opportunities to share, grow, and love together.

So next time someone asks how you are, think twice before you pop out "Fine." Your honesty might open the gate for the other women around to share their struggles and find the support they really need as well. How rewarding is that?

113

CHAPTER THIRTY-FOUR

Loving Your Body Post-Birth

What do you do with your new, more-wobbly-around-the-middle body after birth?

Do you buy new clothes to accommodate the changes or drag about in your hubby's over-sized T-shirts, hoping the signs of your massive life-changing accomplishment (parenthood) will disappear?

I'm not very good at buying myself special things, but I want to tell you the story of once when I did. I ordered a new nursing chemise from Cake Maternity. When it arrived, I was so excited to try it on, but I thought I'd wait for a special occasion and instead I put on my regular bedtime attire: an old T-shirt and plaid pajama pants.

This outfit lasted less than an hour as Miss Baby decided to decorate it with a rather generous helping of milk. This may not have been the special occasion I was hoping for, being far too frequent to be deemed special in any way, but it was reason enough to change, so I decided to try my new nightie on.

I carefully snipped the Cake Maternity label off and put iy on my bathroom shelf. I liked the motto: *Love the Body You're In.* It was symbolic for me as a mom. "Love the body you're in now, as it is, with all its changes," and similarly, "love the life you're in, now, as it is… embrace it and appreciate it… this time with tiny people running about and a chubby baby smiling on your hip or snuggling into your neck with her fuzzy peach head."

This also means embracing and appreciating myself. Not waiting for later to wear the smooth, comfortable chemise that arrived earlier that day, wrapped so prettily in tissue paper as if it was a gift from a friend.

It means saying today is special enough because everyone deserves to be treated with gentleness and love every day, even me, a mom. Perhaps for mothers, who dedicate their lives to making others feel special, it is even more important that we fill our own well and do things that make us feel special also, that we love the body we are in, that we honour it as a place of generous creativity, a place of love and of life.

Yes, this is all a fancy way of saying that we moms deserve pretty pjs! It's because they symbolize something much greater: self-respect, feminine dignity, comfort, and the humility to know we are merely human and need to take care of ourselves in order to be able to serve our families.

While I pondered these things, the baby began to squawk a bit and needed a snuggle dance to settle down. I discovered that the skirt flits about nicely just above the knees as I rocked the baby to sleep and feels elegant and cheerful,as opposed to the tired old plaid pajama pants which drag on the floor, in great danger of picking up stray Cheerios, dust bunnies or stickers.

It so helps that I could order the chemise online rather than trying to buy clothes with my seven kids in tow. Last time I bought pajamas, it was after about two hours of chasing kids through Value Village and another hour of waiting while they tried stuff on in the limited change rooms (my four eldest are girls!).

When it was "my turn" to find pajamas, I just grabbed the first thing I thought could work and hurried to the cashier with my overflowing cart and procession of tired, hungry kids. What I grabbed off the reject rack were soft orange-and-white-striped capri joggers—or as the kids call them, my pirate pants. I usually wear them to bed with my black T-shirt that says "Sarcasm loading…please wait."

Charming right? So given that my options are looking like a sarcastic, washed-up pirate or a sweet, elegant mother, I'm so glad to have my new nursing chemise! Bed is my favourite place at the end of a long day — I may as well dress up for it!

So, ladies, love your body now. It has done amazing things, and the changes are simply heroic battle scars and a new part of your deeper, more meaningful beauty.

CHAPTER THIRTY-FIVE

Losing the Baby Weight

"Hey, you look great!"

"Wow, you don't even look like you had a baby!"

"You just had a baby? No way!"

I heard comments like that a lot after all my births. However, after my third baby, I didn't feel great. I felt like I was carrying extra weight, not from having a baby, but from before her birth. While everyone else complimented my figure, I just wanted to lose the baby weight.

Sometime after Lily's birth, I started dealing with stress by eating. Chocolate solves everything, right? But all that extra chocolate settled around my waist, leaving me with extra weight before I got pregnant with Jade—weight that stayed around after she was born.

One piece of advice I've heard frequently regarding postpartum weight loss is that it took you nine months to gain that baby weight, so give yourself at least nine months to lose it. Your body has gone through a lot, and it won't bounce back overnight. In fact, your body will never be exactly the way it was before giving birth.

Here are few things you can do to help your body heal and recover after pregnancy:

1. Choose healthy options.

This doesn't have to mean giving up all my favourite foods in order to lose weight. It can mean a simple shift in the way I cook so some of my favourite recipes aren't as fattening. For example, I began to cut back on sugar in my baking, use whole wheat breads and pastas, avoid trans fats, eat more fruits and vegetables, etc.

2. Eat slowly.

My dad often talked about this, as meals in my home growing up were a family affair. Dad didn't like it when we gulped back our food and dashed away.

Eating more slowly allows your stomach more time to digest your food—and to inform you that you are full before you overeat. It can be hard to eat at all when you have a baby to hold or toddlers requiring attention, but let their demands help you eat more slowly instead of making you feel rushed into scarfing back your food.

3. Drink lots.

I'm really bad about this, but drinking enough water is important both for weight loss and for breastfeeding. Water can help you feel full, so you are less tempted to snack. I usually avoid juices, as they have extra calories. Instead, I've tried to keep a glass of cold water close to where I'm working or sitting.

Another trick I used was to fill a one-litre water bottle in the morning and try to empty it at least twice during the day. Having the whole water bottle full was a good visual of how much water I'd had during the day.

Adding lemon or cucumber to your water is a good way to get some low-calorie zest in.

4. Choose a lifestyle.

Losing weight isn't going to work if I gain it right back as soon as I finish my diet. I need to change my habits (including how I deal with stress) to lose that belly fat and keep it off. I've seen lots of fad diets in the news, but many of those diets aren't healthy and won't work long-term.

Try to develop healthy habits and ways of eating that you can see yourself doing for years to come instead of trying to stop eating certain things while counting down the days until you can start eating them again.

5. Exercise.

Along with eating healthier, I need to get more active. My husband is always asking me when I'll get back into swimming or biking. I try to get out for a walk with the kids to encourage them to be active as well. It's not the same as a cardio workout, but it's better than nothing.

Some gyms offer "mom and me" classes, which can be a great way to get back into exercising after baby. You're able to get out with your baby and to see other moms. There's a sense of commitment (especially if you pay for the classes at the gym!) that can help you show up there. And you may make some new mom friends at the gym, which is also great!

Another option is to get your husband, a friend, or your mom to take the baby so that you can get some alone time. Maybe that means going for a run for half an hour, heading to the basement to your exercise machine, or dashing off to the gym for a class without baby. Don't feel guilty for taking care of yourself! Your baby will get some great bonding time with another family member and you'll come back feeling stronger both physically and mentally.

6. Get some sleep.

It may seem strange that sleep can affect weight loss, but if you're eating for emotional reasons like me, then having enough sleep can help you feel good about yourself and not grab that extra cookie. Plus, if you're tired, you don't feel like being active. And your body releases stress hormones that can make you gain weight.

Our bodies are wonderful and amazing creations, as I'm reminded by each pregnancy and birth. They stretch and change and grow a baby. It's up to us to take care of our bodies, to respond to cues about sleep and food and exercise and do what's best for ourselves.

Don't try to lose weight just to be skinny again; lose weight because it's part of taking care of yourself postpartum, because it's part of your overall health goals as a mom.

CHAPTER THIRTY-SIX

Be Gentle with Yourself

I'm addicted to my to-do list. My sense of a good or bad day is tied to how much I was able to get done in that day. The problem with this is that many things of value don't fit onto a to-do list—things like taking the baby for a walk or playing peek-a-boo or changing diapers. (Although I have been tempted to list how many times I've changed baby's diaper just to show hubby that I *did* do something all day!)

This to-do list mentality is also problematic in the first few months after giving birth. That time has been given the name of "babymoon" and should be treated as a special break. However, my attitude toward myself is more often "hurry up and heal" so that I can get back to "doing" things like normal.

The postpartum period is a particularly vulnerable and delicate time. Your hormones are raging from pregnancy and giving birth.

The postpartum period is a particularly vulnerable and delicate time. Your hormones are raging from pregnancy and giving birth. No matter how you gave birth—long labour or short, C-section or not—your body went through a grueling process and needs time to heal.

(Sometimes I think women who have C-sections are more aware of this postpartum period; I didn't require stitches after my last three births, so it seems less obvious that my body needs to heal.)

And finally, there's the sleeplessness and adjusting that comes with having a newborn baby around.

My midwives kept repeating their recommendation that women should be on bed rest for at least two weeks after giving birth. They told me that my bleeding would be an indication of whether I was doing too much; if I started bleeding more, I needed to slow down. However, it's often easier to put on a new pad than to lie down for a nap.

Even with my mother-in-law to help for the first two weeks after Pearl's birth and friends dropping off meals, I found myself doing too much. I let myself lie around for the first two days, but then I felt like I needed to be up. I snuck in loads of laundry, though my mother-in-law said she'd do it. I put the ham in the Crock Pot instead of letting her have free reign in the kitchen. I felt guilty when she had to clean up our garbage after a raccoon got into it.

And when she left two weeks after Pearl's birth, I decided we'd get right back into routine. For the first week, that went great. Pearl slept during the mornings and I was able to check off the to-do list.

For the second week, it began to fall apart. Pearl didn't sleep much and I got frustrated that I couldn't put her down to make supper or help Sunshine with her math. Finally, Anna gave me a pep talk and told me to relax and be gentle with myself.

I tried to take things easier. We took an extra week off school after Christmas and then focused on math, adding other subjects as we had time (or a good day with the baby). We were ahead in science and history. Both girls were reading voraciously, so math was the skill they needed the most help with.

I got them to start helping in the kitchen more. I figured this was a good time for them to learn life skills—like taking care of a baby and a home and even taking care of themselves.

Again and again, I found myself having to check my to-do list mentality and give myself grace. When Pearl turned three months old, I found myself thinking once again, "Okay, good, she's getting older so we can get back into a routine." In other words, I can get back to being "productive."

Instead, Pearl had several fussy days that left me staring at my messy house, feeling frustrated and overwhelmed.

If you're like me, I want to say this to you (and myself): be gentle with yourself.

Motherhood is tough. Children are demanding. Babies fuss. Your house will be messy. Your children will misbehave. And you will keep going, and someday (so I'm told) you will look back on these years and remember only the cuteness and the fun, and not the exhaustion and the stress.

So I repeat: until then, be gentle with yourself.

CHAPTER THIRTY-SEVEN

Dealing with Postpartum Hemorrhoids

The birth of a new baby is a wonderful, miraculous event. I'm always amazed when I think about everything my body does over nine months to grow a baby and then, during the hours of labour, to push her out into the world. So many incredible things happen during that time, which is hard on a woman's body. Sometimes, there are unexpected side effects.

I remember having no stomach muscles after Sunshine was born. Even coughing was almost impossible. Nobody warns you about these little things, like how hard it is to sit down for a few days or how the lack of sleep you got during the last month of pregnancy is nothing compared to the lack of sleep with a new baby.

After Lily, though, I faced another problem: hemorrhoids.

These little things aren't really talked about much, but they can be a super pain in the ___ (to borrow a cliché). I mentioned them to my midwife at one of her postnatal visits and she recommended Tucks to me.

Going to the drug store to find these was a bit embarrassing. Especially when the drug store didn't have the product on their shelves and had to order it in. (That's when you really hope for a female pharmacist.)

With Pearl and Joey, my hemorrhoids showed up *before* baby's birth. An unfortunate reality of pregnancy is that all the baby weight pushing down upon our organs can cause discomfort *down there*. Other friends of mine have also found hemorrhoids appearing during the second or third trimesters. These nasty little things are actually related to varicose veins (another pregnancy problem!).

If you're facing these, either before or after baby's birth, here are a few things you can do to treat them.

1. Eat and drink well.

Try to keep your bowel movements soft and regular by drinking lots of water and eating well. Fruits, vegetables and whole grains all help (like the Bran Flakes Anna mentioned in an earlier chapter!). Doula Lori Bregman recommends drinking prune juice with ground flaxseed and taking one tablespoon of coconut oil before bed to help soften stools.

2. Grab an over-the-counter remedy.

Hemoclin is an over-the-counter remedy available at most pharmacies and drug stores as well as online (because really, who wants to be seen picking it up in the store?). It is a clear water-based gel that delivers no pain, no mess, and no stains. It provides cooling relief from anal discomforts (yes, I can confirm this statement).

3. Try witch hazel pads.

Witch hazel has astringent and cooling properties. Soak several cotton pads with witch hazel and apply to your hemorrhoids several times daily. For added comfort, chill the pads in the freezer before applying them. Bregman recommends adding a few drops of vitamin E oil to your pads. You can also buy Tucks, which are pre-made witch hazel pads, at most pharmacies.

4. Make an essential oil compress.

Make a soothing cypress compress for hemorrhoids. *Essential Oils* notes, "Cypress essential oil has a toning effect on the veins... Here it is combined with detoxifying lemon and geranium essential oils, and juniper essential oil, which has an astringent action that is helpful for shrinking ... hemorrhoids." Add three drops each of cypress, lemon, and juniper essential oils with one drop of geranium essential oil to two teaspoons of sunflower oil, then add to a bowl full of cold water. Soak a wash cloth in the water, squeeze out, and sit on the compress for ten minutes.

5. Take a sitz bath.

Keeping your perineal area clean after childbirth is very important and can help with managing hemorrhoids. A soak in warm water once or twice a day may ease discomfort down there. Bregman recommends adding one-quarter cup witch hazel and one-half cup sea salt as well as a few drops of lavender to your bath.

6. Apply baking soda to hemorrhoids.

Baking soda can help reduce itching. Add some to your bath or apply wet or dry directly to your hemorrhoids.

7. Get moving.

Changing position can also reduce hemorrhoids by improving your circulation. Avoid long periods of sitting or standing. Try to move about or vary your positions.

Exercise isn't my favourite thing to do either eight months pregnant or immediately postpartum, but even a small workout can help with hemorrhoids and other problems.

CHAPTER THIRTY-EIGHT

Let's Talk about Postpartum Depression

In my first-year university psychology class, our professor gave us an assignment: find a story in the newspaper that made us ask why someone would do that and research the psychological reasons for it. I spent my next shift at work reading through the papers (Sundays at the gas station were slow). On the very last page of the local paper, I found my story.

A mom of five children was on trial for drowning each of her children, one by one. My heart broke as I read the story, and I asked, "Why? How?" I could hardly wait to get to my professor on Tuesday morning and ask for her opinion on the story though I wasn't sure what psychological reason there could be for this action. My prof took one glance at the story and said, "Postpartum psychosis."

That mom's story, and what I learned about postpartum depression and psychosis, have stayed with me ever since. As a mom, I've developed a lot more sympathy for this other mom. Likely, she had postpartum depression after her first or second baby, but it was unrecognized or untreated. Each pregnancy and birth would have aggravated her depression until it became psychosis after her fifth.

I don't share this story to scare you. For me, this story is a reminder to take care of myself as a mom. It is not selfish to do so. It is not weak to ask for help. I'm not a bad mom if there are moments when my screaming baby makes me want to scream back or when I want to cry in frustration that the baby still won't go to sleep.

The first three months after baby's birth are the hardest. That's why I've included them here as the "fourth trimester." When I had my first daughter, my attitude was that once she was born, life could return to normal. I had my normal clothes back, my normal diet, my normal routines ... or not. I didn't realize how much this small bundle of cuteness would change my life.

None of my babies have been "easy" babies. They prefer bouncing to rocking. They want to sleep with me, not in their crib. They nurse around the clock until they're at least a year old (and often past that). And my last two babies I would certainly describe as colicky.

As a new mom, your body is still recovering from what it went through in pregnancy and childbirth. Your hormones are raging as your body adjusts to breastfeeding. Your emotions are all over the place as you adjust to new motherhood, to taking care of this beautiful, needy little person in your life. That's all normal and okay.

During this time, pay attention to your emotions. Emotions are neither good nor bad; rather, they are like a thermometer that gives us information. It's what we do with that information that matters. Just as you'd glance at the thermometer outside to determine how to bundle up yourself and your baby in an Edmonton winter or whether you need to slap on some sunscreen for a Vancouver summer, use your internal thermometer. Do you need more sleep? Do you need to call a friend? Do you need to talk to your doctor about iron supplements?

Be honest with yourself and with others about your emotions. Talk to your husband about how you are feeling so he can support you. He may also be going through strange and new emotions as he adjusts to new fatherhood (though his emotions likely won't swing to extremes as yours will, aided by hormones). Talk to a friend about how you are feeling (preferably a friend who has had a baby already). Talk to your doctor or midwife, as your exhaustion or other feelings may be caused by something as simple as low iron (especially if you dealt with this during pregnancy).

Emotions are neither good nor bad; rather, they are like a thermometer that gives us information.

One day with Pearl (my fourth), when she'd been screaming at me nonstop for a while no matter what I did, I put her down in her crib and closed the door. As I sank into the rocking chair in the living room, my oldest (then eight) looked at me.

"The baby is crying," she said, expecting me to go pick her up.

"I know," I said.

I didn't have the words or emotional energy to explain to her that right then, I needed a break. I had tried to soothe my baby. I had bounced and rocked and nursed and patted her back and changed her diaper and checked for diaper rash and burped and held and repeated. And she screamed through it.

Nothing I did helped her. It made her screaming feel personal, as if she were saying, "You're a bad mom. I hate you. You're not helping me."

In my head, I knew that wasn't really what was going on. I knew this phase would pass. I knew I just needed a break and that in five minutes her continued screams would tug at my heart and I'd go back and try again. But my emotions—oh, my emotions.

In that tired, frustrated, hormonal state, it's so easy to get caught up in the emotions.

It's okay to put the baby down. It's okay to cry into your pillow. It's okay to call your husband and tell him to bring home some takeout for supper (again). It's okay to ask your mom or your friend to please help with the mountain of laundry. It's okay to let them watch the baby so you can nap.

I wish for you an easy baby, supportive husband, involved grandparents, close friends, and plenty of sleep. If that doesn't happen, then I wish for you the strength to get through these exhausting days, to focus on the beautiful moments, and to ask for help when you need it.

CHAPTER THIRTY-NINE

When Baby is Colicky

Colic is a term that refers to a fussy baby. When I was a first-time mom I didn't like this term, because there's no cause for colic. If baby was fussy, I thought, there had to be a reason for it. Now that I've had five babies, I've realized that sometimes babies do fuss for no reason—or no reason that I can see.

Just as you are adjusting to your new normal, so is your baby. He spent the past nine months tucked snuggly in your womb, warm and wet and quiet and tight. Then, with much squeezing and pushing, he was thrust into this cold, loud, strange world. I'd probably cry too.

When my last baby spent hours screaming at my efforts to help him, I spent a lot of time researching via my phone. It's a bit hard to read while jiggling a wailing baby, but what I found was that there's not much you can do to help colicky babies. Simply know that you are doing the best you can for your baby, and this time will pass. That knowledge helped me to keep rocking (despite the screaming) with a calmer sense that, hey, he's okay and someday he'll stop yelling at me. (And he did).

Swaddling may help your newborn calm down. Get tips from a friend or a YouTube tutorial. You'll need a big, soft swaddling blanket (cotton is better than flannel). There are also newer swaddling systems on the market, but I'd only buy one to start with or see if you can borrow one from a friend to try out. There were a few times when being wrapped tightly seemed to help my babies. Other times, they just got red in the face trying to get their arms free again.

Different motions may help quiet your baby. Remember that when baby was in your womb, he was used to constant motion. Being laid down in a stiff, still crib may feel completely foreign. I found most of my babies preferred bouncing to rocking, but I've honestly tried every motion possible.

Being in a baby carrier can mimic the feeling of being back in the womb for baby. I've worn most of my babies for their first few months, in various carriers. My favourite is the Baby Beluga wrap, which is a soft, stretchy wrap that tucks baby snugly against you. Joey napped best this way while I could still homeschool or cook.

Keeping baby upright can also help with gas or acid reflux. The Beluga Baby and other carriers hold baby upright while properly supporting their back and neck. You may find putting a pillow under one end of your baby's crib mattress helps them sleep better.

When Joey was in his colicky stage, I remembered a friend of mine had sworn by gripe water. I stopped to buy some, but my small local pharmacy had neither gripe water nor Ovol Drops (another over-the-counter colic remedy). At home, I researched both of these and found, to my disappointment, that there's little research to show they help. Instead, it probably just makes mom feel like she's doing something for baby (and that's okay).

Boiron Coccyntal does actually help baby. This homeopathic colic remedy relieves abdominal pain, intestinal cramps, gas, and spasms for baby. Boiron products are available at most pharmacies in Canada and contain none of the "extra" ingredients (sugar, flavoring) that other colic remedies do. I used this for several of my babies and found it effective.

One suggestion I found for colic is that baby's tiny tummy and intestinal system are adjusting to new foods. In the womb, nutrients are delivered to your baby via the umbilical cord, straight to his blood stream. After birth, all your baby's systems have to kick into gear—lungs must start breathing, tummy must start digesting, etc. It made sense to me that Joey's little tummy might get sore as it got used to digesting all the milk he was drinking.

Some babies enjoy car rides. Being strapped into their car seats may help them feel tight and secure, and the vehicle creates its own white noise. If going for a drive calms the baby, go for it! (You can always hit the Starbucks drive-thru for a decaf caramel macchiato while you're out!)

Find some music or a podcast you like while driving or use the time to pray.

Getting out for a walk with baby in a carrier or stroller may help you as much as baby. You may not want to take a screaming baby out for all the neighbourhood to hear but I've found that usually, baby calms down once we're out. Something about fresh air is refreshing for both baby and mom. A little walk, with some new scenery, can help put perspective on life as a mom.

White noise also seemed to help my last three babies. I first discovered this by accident with Jade. I was up late (again) trying to bounce her to sleep. As she continued wailing, I decided I could at least help myself cope better with her screaming by putting on some praise music.

I pressed play on my stereo and began bouncing Jade to the rhythm of the music. As the first song ended, she stopped screaming. As the second song ended, she was asleep, and I turned the stereo off and went to bed. For the next several weeks, that kept working—I never heard more than the first three songs on the CD!

Since then, I've used a variety of other white noise devices and apps. Play with different sounds to see what works for baby. We alternate between classical music ("Fur Elise" on repeat) and nature sounds like "ocean."

Finally, as I mentioned, there may be times when nothing you do seems to help baby and that can feel overwhelming. It's okay to put baby down in his crib or rocker and to walk away for five or ten minutes. Get a cup of tea, eat some chocolate, put on your makeup—do something that makes you feel good about yourself. Then go back and get baby and try again.

CHAPTER FORTY

How to Peacefully Bathe a Newborn

Newborns love being cuddled and cozy, curled up close to mom like they were in the womb. Often their least favourite thing is getting their diaper changed or having a bath, because they feel vulnerable and exposed. They wave their skinny little arms as though they were falling and look very startled.

This means that first baths can be a bit of a scream festival, which is hard on new babies and new mommies and daddies alike. When you're sleep deprived and your hormones are fluctuating, the last thing you want to do is something you know will set off baby alarm bells.

So how do you avoid this? Is there a way to bathe a newborn peacefully? Yes! Please learn from my mistakes and do it the better way.

When I bathed my first daughter, I was so nervous. I didn't want her to get burned by hot water or drown so I only put a few inches of lukewarm water in her baby bathtub. I took forever to bathe her with baby soap before rinsing her off. She hated it, of course, as she was so cold. I hated it too. Her crying made me so upset.

Here are simple steps to a better way:

Fill the baby bathtub really full, almost to the top.

Use really warm water. Not actually hot but much warmer than you would think, remembering that water cools quickly in the small tub.

Cradle the back of your baby's head with your right hand, supporting his body with your arm. To make this easier, I put our baby bath up on the counter. You could use a table instead, with a towel under it. Then you don't have to bend way over and get a sore back.

Lay the other arm on top of baby to hold him secure. If he likes, let him suck your finger to soothe himself. When I did this last time, my newbie got so relaxed he almost fell asleep!

Get your spouse or an older child to gently pour a little water over baby's head (not face) and in those little creases of the neck where milk hides.

Keep the bath brief, about five minutes or so, and don't bother with soap at first. Newborns smell lovely and just need a little dip to freshen up every now and then. You are constantly wiping them during diaper changes or cleaning their little faces with a warm cloth. In my opinion, you don't need to feel pressured to bathe them every day—unless you want to!

Choose a moment when you are fairly relaxed. Ignore the phone or other interruptions and enjoy this cozy moment with your beautiful, precious new mini you!

Have a cozy towel and blanket ready. Follow the bath with a nice snuggle and some warm milk!

CHAPTER FORTY-ONE

Advice for New Parents

We had many friends share their parenting advice with us before Sunshine was born. I'm still grateful for the things they mentioned to us. Much of it was solid, practical advice that has helped us in our parenting journey.

This book is my attempt to pass along some of that pregnancy advice to you. As you move into this wonderful journey, I'd like to add a few parting pieces of advice:

1. Take all advice with a grain of salt.

Yes, this first piece of advice is ironic. As a new parent, you'll find that EVERYONE has some advice for you, from the nurse at the hospital to your family and friends to the lady behind you in the checkout line at the grocery (who will also want to know how much the baby weighed and what her name is).

Your job as a parent is to filter that advice, take the best, and leave the rest. And that's a tough job as a new parent, in the haze of sleeplessness and joy that you're in. You don't want to offend any great-aunts or in-laws and you want to do what's best for your baby.

Just remember that what worked for another parent may not work for you. Every baby and every family is unique, and YOU (and your husband) need to decide what's best for YOU and your baby.

2. Find parent friends.

Looking back on my first few months as a new mom with Sunshine, I've come to see that I was very lonely. Only I didn't know it.

I had Sunshine in the city I'd grown up in, so my parents and in-laws lived close to us. I was also surrounded by my university and childhood friends. However, I was the first among my friends to get married and have kids.

When we moved to Victoria, BC, we immediately got involved with the student community at our local church. After a few months, however, I realized we didn't need other students—we needed other parents. The young singles we were hanging out with faced a completely different reality than we did in taking classes. We switched churches, found some supportive fellow parents, and that made a huge difference in our years as students.

As new parents, you need friends who are also parents, who get what it's like to be up at night with a crying baby and won't care if you come to visit with spit-up on your shoulder.

If you've recently moved or had kids before the rest of your friends, then you'll need to find new friends. Check out your local community center, church, or library for a mom's group and reach out to other parents.

3. Ask for and accept help.

I've mentioned this is really hard for me to do, but as parents, you really do need the community around you. I was given this advice as a new mom with Sunshine and mostly ignored it. Don't make my mistake! Parenting a newborn is tough; you need help. That might mean asking your husband to wash the dishes or your mother-in-law to wash the laundry, or it might mean asking someone to take the baby so you can rest or bring you meals so you don't have to cook.

When we had Jade, so many friends brought us food that I didn't have to cook for a week. They taught me the meaning of community and helping new parents. So if someone says, "Let me know how I can help you," smile and say, "It would be great if you could drop a meal off for us after the baby is born."

4. Buy things as you need them.

There are tons of lists of must-have items for new babies and new parents. It can be overwhelming to think about everything you need.

The truth is, you really don't need very much. Babies are simple and have simple needs. I suggest getting the basics, like clothes and blankets, diapers and a diaper bag, and a car seat and then getting the rest as you decide you need it.

For example, we bought a crib and then a cradle for Sunshine only to find she refused to sleep in either. We co-slept with her for the first several months, then slowly transitioned her into the cradle by our bed and finally into her own crib when she was about six months old. Lily and Jade did the same thing, but we didn't even use the crib with Pearl or Joey.

I didn't get a baby monitor until we had Jade (when we had a two-story townhouse, so it was harder to hear the baby crying). We also didn't have a baby gate until Jade (as every other house we lived in was single-story).

If you are short on space, you don't need a ton of baby furniture. A friend of ours showed us how she had a diaper basket and changing pad stowed away behind the couch. When the baby needed changing, she pulled out the basket, spread the pad on the floor, and changed the baby. No worries about baby rolling off the table!

I adopted a similar system when Jade was born. I just changed her on the end of our bed and kept the diapers and wipes in a dresser drawer within arms' reach.

Think creatively and you'll find solutions.

5. Give yourself grace.

Parenting is tough. Being a new parent is a huge learning curve. (Seriously—your first baby is your hardest. It gets easier with the next.) So give yourself some grace as you figure this out. Sleep. Pray. Admire baby toes. Let go of the little things, like laundry and dishes, which will get done someday.

I thought I was prepared to become a mom because I'd babysat for years, even for small babies. New motherhood was still a huge jolt for me. Breastfeeding was hard. Sunshine wanted to be held all the time. I couldn't get the laundry or dishes done.

As a perfectionist dedicated to my to-do list, that felt horrible. Just sitting around holding a baby all day made me feel unproductive. But that's what Sunshine needed right then and it didn't last very long.

You are an awesome parent. Tell yourself that. Tell your spouse that. You'll get this parenting thing done (probably not overnight) and someday you'll laugh about the sleep deprivation and other things you worried about. For now, take care of yourself and your baby and let go of the rest.

Birth Stories

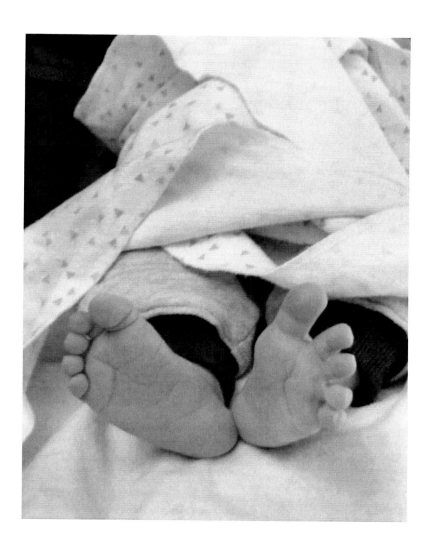

CHAPTER FORTY-TWO

Anna's Hospital Water Birth

First births are always rather epic and intense. This was the case with my first, but I now realize how much better it could have been. I am going to share with you four of my nine births so you can journey with me through them and hopefully learn, a lot sooner than I did, how to advocate for yourself and get the support you need during and after labour.

The first mistake I made was going it too much alone. It was around 11:30 pm when my contractions started becoming regular, while still about ten to fifteen minutes apart. I called my friend and more experienced mom Laura to see what she thought. She agreed this seemed like the real deal, so I began packing my hospital bag (finally!).

After I packed the bag, my husband and I tried to get some sleep, figuring we would wake up if things intensified. I did, a few hours later, as contractions got more painful and closer together. My whole body felt awful; I wanted to throw up and had terrible cramps.

I went to the bathroom and my body cleared out everything but the baby. I didn't know it, but this is called going through transition. I should have woken up my husband, but it was 2:30 in the morning.

Instead, I had a bath, trying to seek comfort in the warm water. After a while, I dried off and went to the living room, wrapped in a big quilt. Now it was more like 4:30 a.m., and I was starting to think I should call the midwives ... but it was sooo early!

By the time I was about to try calling, my husband found me on the living room floor, moaning and wrapped in the quilt. We called the midwives, though I could hardly speak through the contractions, which were about five minutes apart. They said labour was progressing and to meet them at the hospital ASAP.

Next we called my dad to come pick us up and drive us there, as we didn't own a car. He hopped into what seemed like an extremely long shower and finally arrived.

By this time, I was in a lot of pain, and it was not a fun 6:30 a.m. car ride. Happily, the midwife was waiting for us at the hospital, and quickly got us checked into a private room. I remember her offering me a birthing ball to roll on, which was supposed to help; it did not.

Instead, she ran a hot bath, and it was a great relief to sink into the warm embrace of water, knowing it was now safe to have my baby. The contractions were so strong and were now replaced with an irresistible urge to push.

"Do you want to come out to have the baby?" the midwife asked.

"No way!"

I felt a great pressure below, like I was going to have diarrhea, but the nurses said it was the baby's head. There was a terrible burning feeling as she crowned, but I grunted through it and gave in to my body's desire to push like crazy. And then, after several pushes, out slipped the head, then shoulders of my tiny miracle, and she was scooped up onto my chest to admire.

That first glimpse of her tiny face, little scrunched up eyes and miniature mouth, and the feeling of her tiny warm body, wet and waxy from her lifetime in the womb, is indescribable. Time stops and you feel the universe begin to orbit around your new little daughter or son. Your heart now has a face and beats outside yourself.

After some moments to snuggle her and grin with amazement at my husband, we were brought back to reality by the nurses' need to check her vitals and record APGAR scores. I reluctantly handed her over and was guided by my midwife into the more prosaic duty of pushing out the placenta.

Happily, a few pushes were enough for this job, and it slipped out more easily than the baby did. Then I was helped out of the tub, into a hospital gown and up onto the bed. Back then, it was standard for the nurse to bathe the newborn right away rather than give them skin-to-skin time on mama's chest. I had to listen to the tiny cries of rage my daughter emitted about this indignity.

At this time, my OB, who was also on my case because of my cholestasis, a pregnancy liver condition (see Chapter 6), came to check my birthing tears, and said she needed to do some stitches. This was not fun.

Everything hurt, and the laughing gas they offered didn't seem to do anything. The bleeding wouldn't let up either, so she realized there were in fact large internal tears caused by my baby holding her tiny, sharp hands up on her head during birth. There's a reason heads are round and smooth!

So after my natural, medication-free water birth, I was wheeled off to the operating room for an epidural after all. I remember nervously leaning over a chair so they could give me the needle, but I honestly can't remember the pain, so it can't have been that bad, at least not after what I'd been through already that morning.

After a few minutes, everything belly down became warm and comfortable, and I stopped feeling pain. I even cheerfully chatted with the OB and told her silly stories about my pet cat as she sewed me up.

During this time, my husband, James, got to glory in being a new dad and to hold his tiny towel-wrapped bundle for an hour or two. By the time the nurses brought me to the recovery room and handed me a paltry snack of cheese and crackers and a juice box (I was starving!), James was quite attached to her. I remember him requesting "his" baby back again after I had a cuddle or nursed her that day! Well, really!

But then again, I'd held her inside for nine months, and it was adorable to see him gazing at her with such wonder and delight.

We stayed a night or two in the hospital to recover before heading home with our baby girl—attentive, nervous, and overjoyed new parents.

I remember feeling unsure about making my own decisions and pressured by others about the timing of recovery, when to take my first walk or first outing with the stroller on the bus, etc. Many well-meaning people had strong opinions about how and when things should be done.

Don't let yourself be rushed! Have confidence in yourself and listen to your gut. Go gently and savour these first magical days—better too slow than too fast when recovering from the major event of birth.

CHAPTER FORTY-THREE

Bonnie's Hospital Birth with a Midwife

My husband's friends began calling us on Saturday to ask if there was a baby yet. It was my due date, and they were excited about our first baby.

"Sorry," we said. "I guess we forgot to tell the baby that today was the due date."

We were out browsing baby stores, comparing prices and thinking about what we'd need in the next few months. Baby was being shy, my husband said.

Early the next morning, I woke up with a burning backache, and fumbled for my body pillow before falling back asleep. In a few minutes, the backache returned, and I adjusted the pillow and drifted back to sleep.

When the backache returned for the third time, it finally occurred to me that maybe this was labour. With the fourth contraction, I thought to start timing them. Seven minutes apart.

I was debating how soon to wake my husband and head for the hospital when the next one came, and he woke up to ask what was wrong.

"I think the baby's coming," I said.

He rolled over to hold me, and the warmth of his body helped ease the pain. He asked how far apart the contractions were and then sprang into action.

While he gathered the things we needed for the hospital, I managed to dress and tried to deal with each contraction. They were definitely strong and five minutes apart when we got into the car. My husband called our parents on the way, and just before 8:00 a.m. on Sunday morning, we were signed into the hospital.

The nurse checked on me and the baby and then mostly left us to ourselves. I moved from the shower to the tub to pacing around the room to the shower again while my husband coached me through the pain and reminded me to drink lots. Most of what I ate or drank, I threw up with the stronger contractions.

By noon, I was tired and just wanted to curl up in the bed, but the pain wouldn't let me.

When the nurse came in to check on us once and asked how far apart the contractions were, my husband started timing them again. They were two minutes apart while I was in the shower. To his great alarm, my contractions slowed when I moved back into the tub.

He'd stare at the clock, muttering, "There should be one coming soon," and when another minute passed before I sat up and began rocking with the pain, he'd get anxious. Labour wasn't supposed to slow down, he thought.

I knew the tub was relaxing me and slowing things, but I was so tired. However, when the pain wasn't helped by the warm water, I got out and began pacing. Then transition (the hardest part of labour) hit.

I moaned and said I couldn't do it anymore while my husband and the nurse kept telling me I was doing great. I knew we'd agreed we weren't going to use pain medication, so there was nothing to do but keep going and focus on the thought of the baby being here soon.

The midwife arrived as I began pushing, crouched on the bed with my head buried against a pillow while I fought the pain and the exhaustion. At first, each push hurt, but then I just wanted the baby in my arms. I could feel her moving through my body with each push, but it seemed agonizingly slow. The midwife offered gentle suggestions, watching and guiding, while the nurse and my husband stood by to help.

When the baby crowned, my husband let me know, adding, "And baby has lots of hair!" I was in "labourland," my eyes closed, just focused on getting that baby out. Just get past the head, I thought. Push, push, push. And then finally I felt the baby slither out and the midwife caught her and put her on my chest—slimy, wet, bloody, but beautiful.

My husband and I stroked her while she wailed her protests at this strange new world. It may be cliché, but it was true that right then nothing else mattered. She was there and the pain was worth it.

I held her until the placenta came, and then my husband watched while the nurse cleaned her up. The midwife took care of me and helped me try breastfeeding my little daughter, who had finally calmed down. Then her daddy got a chance to hold her while I hobbled into the shower to clean up.

We stayed in the hospital overnight. My mom was able to come visit us at the hospital and hold her first granddaughter while my husband slipped out for a bit. At night, we piled into the hospital's Murphy bed together.

Sometime in the middle of the night, Sunshine woke up and I attempted to feed her again. Both of us being new to it, we were soon frustrated. I began to cry, saying, "Just eat!" as I held her tiny mouth up to my bulging breast. My crying woke up my husband, who sat up and patted my back. "You're doing great," he said, and even though he couldn't do anything more than that to help us, I felt calmer and she soon ate.

We were supposed to remain in the hospital for twenty-four hours after Sunshine's birth. By early afternoon, we were ready to go. Sunshine was dressed in her going-home outfit—a white-and-yellow sleeper we'd picked out for her and a fleece hat a co-worker had given me—and we'd practiced getting her into her car seat. We watched the clock, waiting for 3:00 p.m. and our midwife's approval to leave.

Finally, she dropped by, checked me and Sunshine, and gave us the all-clear to return home as a new little family.

CHAPTER FORTY-FOUR

Anna's Naturally Induced Water Birth

My second birth was more calm and orderly than my first, partly because I (Anna) had more trust in my midwives after knowing them for longer and partly because I had more confidence in myself.

As with my first pregnancy, I suffered from cholestasis, which can make your blood quite polluted as your liver fails to eliminate toxins. This uncomfortable, itchy condition is somewhat correlated with stillbirth, especially towards the end of the pregnancy, so it was essential to have my baby a few weeks early. I was so afraid of being induced during my first pregnancy and possibly ending up with a C-section, that I was not very open to speeding up my baby's arrival.

With my second, my midwife and I had a plan and were able to use natural methods like exercise, spicy food and a labour cocktail (see Chapter 27) to help my baby come two weeks early.

My mother arrived on a Friday to stay with us and take care of my toddler during labour. I went to my midwife appointment and received a stretch and sweep to stimulate my cervix. It produced some painful contractions and helped soften my cervix but didn't bring on labour.

On Sunday, the planned birthing day, I walked to morning Mass, prayed for a safe labour, and came home.

Shortly after lunch, my friend Patty joined us to hang out and be ready to drive us to the hospital at any moment. The midwife came and gave me another stretch and sweep, and then we prepared the labour cocktail, a lemonade with some powerful drops of lemon verbena oil.

Sounds funny, but after sipping my "cocktail" on the couch for an hour or so, regular contractions started up and off we went to the hospital mid-afternoon.

I knew I wanted a water birth again, so we started filling the large birthing tub at the hospital right away. It was so nice to be in it sooner than with my first and to not have things feel so hectic and rushed as they had been then. My husband sat next to the tub, passing me sips of lemonade. It was rather surreal; somehow after already having a baby, the imminent arrival of another seemed even more of a miracle rather than less.

My midwife Liz coached me through labour and taught me to sway about during the strong contractions, comforted by the ease of movement in the deep, hot water. She also helped me to resist the urge to push until I was fully dilated and to pace myself once I was. She showed me how to apply gentle counter pressure on my perineum when the pushing made it sting and to breathe through pushing contractions to take it slow.

All this excellent help resulted in much less physical trauma, as it prevented tearing. No need to sit on a cushion for a month after birth this time!

My second baby was born late that afternoon. Our halfway ultrasound had been a little early, so the technician wasn't allowed to tell us the gender. After the baby slipped out into the warm water, I was so busy cuddling my newborn that I forgot to even check the gender.

"Is it a boy or a girl?" I asked after a few minutes, and, laughing, we checked. Another precious daughter!

Everything was easier this time, as we had done it before, so nursing was no problem. We actually went home that same night around 9:30 p.m., as I was anxious about my toddler, who had never been away from us at night. I still considered my twenty-two-month-old such a baby I hadn't weaned her, and she depended on me to get to sleep.

When we got home, our toddler was happy with her Nanna and likely would have been fine if I had stayed to recover at the hospital. She was excited to see her baby sister, but as she got more tired, she wanted me to lie down and cuddle her. I was then torn between nursing her to sleep and feeding my newborn, who also began to object to not being in her mama's arms.

I'm not sure who cried more than night—the toddler, the baby, or (at least on the inside) me!

146

Long story short, I highly recommend weaning one child before having another! With the help of my mother-in-law, who came to visit, I managed to wean my eldest after a few months. Though I went on to have seven more children, I never tandem nursed again.

My third birth was quite similar to my second, except there was a slightly larger space (twenty-six months instead of twenty-two) than between my first and second babies, and I had weaned my second child before my third came.

After taking a labor cocktail to induce labour two weeks early, my third daughter was born at 9:30 p.m., also on a Sunday. Although the nurses asked if I wanted to go home that very night, I stayed in the hospital. My two older girls were having a sleepover for about a week with their Nanna and Opa, so I had time to heal and recover peacefully before attempting things like picking up my toddler.

CHAPTER FORTY-FIVE

Bonnie's Second Baby Arrives before the Doctor

When the first tightening across my abdomen hit on Friday night, I glanced at the clock, just in case. 4:30 p.m. Over the next hour, the cramps were regular enough to keep me hoping it was labour and sporadic enough that I kept forgetting the time of the last one—ten or fifteen minutes apart and not very strong. That was the start of Lily's birth.

I began gathering the last few things we needed for the birth and finished making supper. After supper, my hubby picked up the phone to call his sister about getting together. I said, "I wouldn't do that."

He gave me a puzzled look and I added, "We might be in labour."

He hung up the phone. Then he wanted to know how far apart the contractions were. He called his parents to warn them we might be calling them later to watch Sunshine. We walked down to check the mail. Contractions were about ten minutes apart.

His parents came when we got back from the mail and picked up Sunshine. After they left, we checked our email and Facebook. My hubby's longtime buddy called and asked, "You're still pregnant?"

I said, "Yep," grinning. Not for long now!

He talked to my husband for an hour or so while I read and wrote in my journal, pacing whenever a contraction hit. When they got off the phone, I called my doula to tell her we were in labour. Around 9:00 p.m., I called her again to say she should come, since she had a forty-five minute drive. Then we watched *Mythbusters* while timing contractions (as per Anna's tips in chapter 27 for encouraging labour to start).

After the doula arrived, we went for another walk. It was a beautiful summer evening. The sky was full of stars we could just barely see past the streetlights. We chatted lightly, getting to know each other.

By the time we got back, contractions were getting stronger and closer. My husband put our bags in the car and asked me a dozen times if we needed anything else. My doula braided my hair, rubbed my back, and tried to help me relax through contractions. I thought about how I'd wanted this to get started and now I just wanted it over.

Just before midnight, my contractions were three minutes apart and very strong. We decided to head for the hospital. I had a contraction in the car just before we got there, another as we walked into Emergency, and another while we talked to the receptionist. She had a long list of questions for us before we could go into the room.

Once in the room, the nurse wanted to hook me up to the Electronic Fetal Monitor. I tried to explain that my doctor had agreed I could pass on it when the doula reminded me of my birth plan. She found it for the nurses and they used the Doppler to get the baby's heartbeat.

When the nurse did an exam, she said I was only one centimeter dilated. I was disappointed. When we'd gotten to the hospital for Sunshine's birth, I'd already been six centimeters along. I wondered if moving from home to the hospital had made me close up again. I paced through a few more contractions, then asked to get in the shower. Perhaps the water would help my body relax.

The nurse wanted to put an IV in first but couldn't find my vein. Finally, after several contractions, she got the needle into my hand, wrapped it up in a plastic bag, and I climbed into the warm water.

My husband and the doula were back to timing contractions, so I had to yell at them each time one started or ended. Then the nurse had more questions for me—was I allergic to anything? Had I been sick lately? On and on the questions went.

Finally the water wasn't helping anymore, so I got out. I thought things were taking longer than they had with Sunshine, especially when the nurse did another exam and I was only five centimeters dilated. The second baby was supposed to be easier, and it wasn't.

For a while, I rocked on the ball or leaned on my husband through the contractions. They began getting stronger and I began howling through them—Ina May Gaskin or somebody had said there was a connection between the openings of the body. Between contractions, I dropped into the big recliner and zoned out. I tried to relax, to focus on the baby, to think about opening so the baby could move down.

Then two contractions came back-to-back and I thought, "No, you can't do this to me! I need a break!"

The nurses told me to focus and my doula told me to breathe calmly. I had my break after that contraction and with the next one I wanted to push.

I mumbled that to the nurses and they phoned the doctor. He only lived five minutes from the hospital, they'd assured me, so he'd be right over. They told me to get up on the bed and not to push yet.

I had reached down to see how things were going, and I thought, "How am I supposed to get up there with a bag of water between my legs?" Between the next contractions, I managed to climb up and my waters broke.

Then, as the nurses scrambled around to find the squatting bar I'd requested and get into their gowns, I had to push. My doula told me to blow, to focus on her, and everyone yelled "don't push yet" and I tried not to but my body was pushing anyways. The bar never made it into place; I turned around and, hanging onto the doula and my husband, kept trying not to push while the nurse who had never managed to get gowned began to catch the baby.

I remembered the burning ring of fire, but when they said the head was out, I was surprised. Then came the order not to push again while she checked the baby's head; and when they said push, I couldn't. Somehow, I mustered enough strength and muscle to give that last push, and the baby slithered, purple and wet, onto the bed.

As they rubbed her down, I tried to sit and said, "Let me hold her. Let me hold her." She wailed and flailed her arms and finally she was clean enough that the nurses let me pick her up. She calmed immediately and the nurses kept rubbing her down and waited until the doctor came before cutting the cord.

He was concerned about my bleeding. The nurses told him I'd declined the oxytocin shot unless necessary. He agreed to see if the bleeding would stop on its own. My doctor had gone on holiday and told us that Dr. N would be covering for her, but this was Dr. V, a tall man with a Dutch accent.

They wrapped us up in warm blankets and I tried to get Lily to nurse. Dr. V stitched me up and then, while my husband took Lily, I went for a shower. It was quick, as I was tired.

Finally, both of us were tucked into the bed, clean and wrapped in warm blankets, for a much-needed rest.

Lily's birth took just as long as Sunshine's, to my great disappointment. She arrived exactly one week after her due date, just before 5:00 a.m. on Saturday morning.

CHAPTER FORTY-SIX

Bonnie's Third Birth: When Contractions Take a Break

On my due date, my husband and I took his mom for high tea at the Empress Hotel in Victoria, BC. In the evening, we went for a belated sixth birthday dinner for Sunshine with friends of ours. I thought perhaps having two reservations would convince baby to come, but nope. The next day, I came down with a bad cold and spent the day in bed.

On Monday, I still felt exhausted. Lily and I saw the doctor about our colds, then went to see my midwife, who told me women rarely go into labour when they're sick. So I had to get myself healthy. My midwife also gave me two doses of verbena oil to help encourage labour, and I took those on Wednesday and Thursday.

Nothing happened. My husband's parents (who'd come for Sunshine's birthday and planned to stay and help with baby) came down with the cold and decided to return home.

On Monday, I was back at my midwife's for the second just-in-case-the-baby-doesn't-come appointment. They asked how I was feeling and I said, "Impatient." Mostly because everybody I ran into asked me, "No baby yet?"

Nope, obviously no baby yet! So my midwife swept my membranes and sent me home with a labour cocktail.

On Tuesday morning, I drank my cocktail (active ingredient: castor oil) and waited. I soon felt nauseous from the castor oil and tired from the Gravol (which only took the edge off the nausea). I spent a few hours lying on the couch with Sunshine (who also wasn't feeling well) watching Lily play. Around 1:30, light contractions started about five minutes apart.

My husband got home from his university classes around 2:00 p.m. At 3:00 p.m., I decided to go to my fiction workshop, as my contractions were still light. I spent the workshop timing contractions and discussing the plots of the four stories we were critiquing and then slipped out right after and came home.

My husband made supper, so we ate together. Afterwards, he took the girls over to my friend Val's for the night. (One of my biggest questions in preparing for a homebirth was where the girls would go while I had the baby. Thankfully, they were happy to have a sleepover and Val was happy to have them.)

I let my midwife know I was in labour, and we called our parents. As I was talking to my mom, I paced up and down the hallway and my contractions started getting harder and three minutes apart. I hung up on Mom and called the midwife again. She arrived around 9:00 p.m.

Then we waited, and talked, and waited…

My husband and I went for a walk in the drizzling rain. I bounced on my yoga ball a bit. And the contractions seemed to slow down.

The second midwife arrived as I was taking another dose of verbena oil to encourage the contractions to speed up again. I was disappointed; I'd wanted this to be a short, quick labour, and I had three ladies sitting in my house just waiting for the baby to come.

By 11:30 p.m., my contractions had petered out to nothing. My midwives got called by another woman in labour. So I had a nap for an hour while they went to check on the other mom.

At 1:00 a.m., my midwife came to listen to the baby's heartbeat. I was lying on my side in bed when suddenly I felt a pop, a warm gush and after a few seconds, I realized my water had broken. I stepped into the shower while my midwives changed my sheets.

My contractions got stronger then, still five minutes apart, but I had to breathe deeply through them. After about half an hour, I got out of the shower and put my TENS unit back on. However, most of the pain was across my abdomen, so I'm not sure the TENS helped.

For the rest of labour, I was in my room as I'd planned. I would do deep squats beside the bed when a contraction hit then lie down and rest between contractions. All three midwives were back, sitting quietly with me and checking the baby occasionally with the Doppler.

When the pain started getting bad, I knew I was getting close to the end, but I still felt like crying—it was hard. I looked at the clock at 2:30 a.m. and thought to myself, "I want this baby out by 3:00." I knew I shouldn't set deadlines like that, so I went back to labouring and tried to ignore the clock.

The urge to push came slowly. I felt like I had to poop at first, but I knew that wasn't enough yet, so I kept waiting. Then something switched and I got onto the bed on all fours. I expected pushing to be quick and easy, like it had been with Lily, but it wasn't.

My first pushes felt like they did nothing. Then everything hurt and I could feel the baby coming out, but it seemed so slow—and the urge to push went away. So we waited, with baby halfway out, until the next urge to push came.

I had no energy left. Everything hurt and it was so hard.

Then, with a last push with all the strength I could muster, the baby squiggled out between my knees at 3:00 a.m. My midwives helped me lie down and hold her, while they rubbed her and we waited for the placenta to come. We discovered she was a girl and picked her name—we'd been playing with three or four names, but one seemed to suit her now that she was here.

I wrapped up in a blanket and tried nursing her, then my midwife checked her over. They packed up their stuff (although I don't remember that) and we fell asleep. This was the best part of my homebirth—simply being able to crash afterwards, in the comfort of my own bed, without the noise of a hospital or nurses checking on me or wondering when we'd get to go home.

The baby nursed like a pro—I was seriously amazed at how easy breastfeeding her was. We slept until 11:00 a.m., when I got up to have a quick shower while she was still sleeping. I slept for the afternoon while my husband had to go to class.

Just before supper, my husband went to get the older girls. They came back with a hot supper from Val as well as balloons and flowers. Lily walked in the door and saw me holding the baby and said, "Wow, baby!" Later, she ran circles around the living room, saying, "I'm so happy! I'm so excited!" Sunshine wanted to hold the baby right away; she sat on the couch and put her arms in a circle.

CHAPTER FORTY-SEVEN

Anna's Fourth Birth: Listen to Your Body

My fourth labour was natural instead of induced, because for once I didn't get cholestasis and there was no need to be induced. It seems that part of the cause of this happy circumstance was eating Bran Flakes faithfully everyday day, as my OB recommended, to help prevent my body from getting plugged up and reabsorbing toxins. This was a mercy as my third and fourth daughters were my closest together at only fourteen months apart.

Around 6:30 a.m. on the day before my due date, I awoke to a painful contraction. It felt different than the usual Braxton Hicks or practice contractions that help the body prepare for labour. This felt like the real deal.

About twenty minutes later came another. I got up at 7:00 a.m. and told my husband labour was starting. He seemed to think there was plenty of time to spare, as the contractions weren't close together, and hopped in the shower.

By the time he came out around 7:30 a.m., I was sitting on the floor in great pain. I called the midwives and had a hard time talking during contractions, which were much closer together, maybe five minutes apart or so. They said to come to the hospital ASAP.

We called my dad, who lived nearby and was planning to come watch our kids while we were at the hospital. About forty-five minutes later, he was still not there! Labour was picking up even more, and we decided I better go ahead.

My upstairs neighbour kindly drove me to the hospital on her way to dropping her kids off at school. My midwife admitted me and put me in a waiting room on a bed. James, who planned to catch a cab after my dad arrived, was still not there. It turned out the lock on Dad's scooter has rusted shut and he had to take the bus.

When James finally arrived at almost 9:00 a.m., I was almost ten cm dilated!

"Would you like to walk up to the birthing room?" the nurse asked.

"No way!" I could hardly move from the strength of the contractions. The nurse helped me into a wheelchair instead, and the midwife took me up in the elevator, encouraging me gently while I tried not to have the baby right there. There was no time to fill the tub for a water birth, so they helped me onto the bed.

The nurse left to register me in the room at the nurse's desk down the hall, and the midwife suddenly said, "James, hold her leg up!" The baby was coming, nurse or no nurse. By the time she arrived back in the room, my new little daughter was in my arms.

She was my biggest baby at almost eight pounds, and was plump, rosy and full of life. I remember she nursed from about 9:30 a.m. till almost lunchtime! While all this nursing was good to release oxytocin and help my uterus contract, it gave me terrible after-cramps. I was in such pain that I kept throwing up. The cold egg salad sandwich they brought for my lunch did not help. I was not feeling clear or strong enough to advocate well for myself and to ask for stronger pain meds or some warm food. The midwife did bring me hot tea with milk and honey, which helped restore my blood sugar a bit.

So what are my big take-aways from birth four?

Trust your body and go to the hospital when *you* feel you need to. Don't let others, even your husband, make you doubt yourself. Better early than late.

After-cramps get worse after multiple babies. Even if you have a medication-free birth, do yourself a favour and get stronger pain meds afterward (more than the usual Advil-Tylenol combo). You've been through enough, and it's better to relax and enjoy your baby than to feel more pain when you're already exhausted.

Bring your own favourite takeout or order it in! The time of day doesn't matter; you deserve a nice hot meal! This is not a time to be shy about asking to be taken care of well.

CHAPTER FORTY-EIGHT

Bonnie's Fourth Arrives on Her Due Date

I tried not to count too much on my due date with my fourth baby after having two babies go past their due dates. Even my midwives seemed to think I'd go "late" again, but still, I made sure everything was ready by that date. As my due date approached, I went to bed each night thinking "maybe tomorrow" and woke up telling myself "okay not today."

On Sunday night, I packed my hospital bag (a just-in-case measure), with my almost-three-year-old wondering hopefully if we were going on a choo choo train or airplane. I baked two quiches for supper, because we had lots of ham and eggs, and thought as I put one quiche in the fridge, "Okay, three casseroles in the freezer and one in the fridge— good time to have a baby."

At 2:30 a.m. on Monday morning, I felt a cramp across my abdomen that was definitely more than a Braxton Hicks. "Yes. It's today," I thought. Due date!

During contractions, I stood up and squatted or rocked through them, praying to take my mind off the pain. Between contractions, I lay down and slept. By 7:00 a.m., my contractions were getting closer to five minutes apart and I'd had one strong enough to make me throw up.

My husband's alarm went off during one contraction. He noticed my deep breathing and asked, "Baby?"

I said, "Yep," and he threw off the covers and said, "I'll call Val."

My friend Val from Victoria had offered to come to Vancouver to watch the older three girls while I had the baby. My husband let her know I was in labour, and she said she'd be on the next ferry.

Then I called my midwife. Jade woke up, so I went to get her, noticing as I passed Lily's room that her light was already on too.

"Lily wake me up," Jade told me indignantly.

"Do you want to go play with her?" I said, lifting her down from her crib and trying to breathe through a contraction. She said yes. Sunshine asked me something about the day and when I said no, she asked why.

I said, "Because the baby is coming today," and Jade said, "Yay!"

Worried the girls' waking up would slow down my labour as it had slowed down when the midwives arrived during Jade's birth, I urged them to get dressed and eat breakfast while I messaged another friend of mine. She lives five minutes from us and had offered to watch the girls if we needed help. I figured she could take the girls until Val could get here. Then I went back to my room to pace and pray through contractions.

By 8:30 a.m., my midwife arrived and my husband whisked the girls out the door. My midwife checked my blood pressure and baby's heartbeat (both good), set up her things, then offered to check my dilation.

I was a bit uncertain about this, as it had been disappointing with both Jade and Lily to feel like I was far along in labour only to find out I was hardly dilated. But I let her check between contractions and was happy that I was already seven centimeters. Things were moving faster, as I'd hoped.

My husband made it back again, and the backup midwife arrived as well. My midwife offered to break my water to speed up labour and again, I agreed. I've hoped with all of my labours since my first that they'd go faster, but my first three labours had all been ten hours long.

Then it was just waiting. Contractions continued and I squatted through them or sat on the edge of the bed, resting and waiting for the next one.

Pushing seemed to take forever with this baby. With Lily, it had been so easy—an urge I couldn't control, two hard pushes, and she was here. Even with Jade, pushing had been almost automatic even as I tried to slow it down and listen to my midwives (and not tear).

This time, I kept waiting for that urge, which never seemed to come. My midwife suggested the birthing stool, but that hurt worse, so I moved back to the bed and continued waiting on all fours, as I'd birthed Jade.

Finally, I was pushing. Slowly, painfully, the baby moved down. Then, with a gush of more water, she slithered out. I flopped down on the bed and took her in my arms, and the midwives wrapped us both in a towel. She was quiet, looking up at me. I got my husband to check whether she was a boy or a girl. The placenta slid out and my midwife assured me I hadn't torn again this time.

Then the shivering began. I went from sweating through contractions just before she was born to shaking uncontrollably after she was born. (The one thing I miss about homebirths is the heated blankets at the hospital.)

My husband took the baby for a bit, and the midwives checked her over while I went for a hot shower. Then we stripped the wet sheets off the bed, and I curled up with our newest little girl.

I spent the rest of the day sleeping and feeding baby Pearl. My husband picked up Val at the ferry at noon, and she took the girls out for the afternoon. He cleaned up a bit around the house and got me juice and snacks.

The girls came home at bedtime, excited to meet their little sister. Jade was actually the first to ask to hold her, putting her arms out. We let them each have a turn and took pictures and videos and then sent them off to get ready for bed.

My mother-in-law arrived on Tuesday to help for a week or so. I worked on resting and enjoying the "babymoon" while the girls got lots of Grandma time.

CHAPTER FOURTY-NINE

Bonnie's Fifth Birth Story

Sunshine looked at the calendar on Saturday, December 9, and said, "Baby is coming today!" I laughed.

I'd written "EDD" on the calendar and explained that it meant "*estimated* delivery date," but apparently the girls still expected their brother on his due date. Lily and Jade were equally disappointed that Baby was still keeping us waiting by the end of the day.

I worked on rearranging the girls' room, as we'd found a new dresser for them to replace the bookshelves and cubes we'd been using. By the end of the weekend, I had cleaned the bathrooms, finished the girls' room, and made sure all the baby stuff was ready. We also took the girls to the sledding hill.

On Monday morning, I decided it was time to give Baby a few hints about arriving. I called Anna to ask her for her labour cocktail recipe and then planned a spicy East Indian meal for dinner. I added a pineapple to my online grocery order for good measure.

When the hospital called to book an ultrasound for me in case Baby hadn't shown up before Friday, I said yes. I had no intention of spending my morning down at the hospital checking up on Baby; I wanted to be holding him.

At noon, we ran to the airport to pick up my mom, who was coming to visit for a week. She helped me run a few errands on the way home.

About mid-afternoon, as we drove, I felt something across my tummy that made me glance at the clock. It was a bit harder than the Braxton Hicks contractions I'd been having for the past weeks, but not quite labour yet.

We picked up my grocery order and headed home. By the time we got there, I knew I wouldn't need the pineapple, castor oil, or spicy East Indian food.

While Mom and I danced back and forth in the kitchen, making chicken tikka masala and cauliflower coconut curry, I tried to time contractions. They were still irregular.

In the evening, I walked Sunshine to her dance class (despite her protests), as it gave me a chance to shake Baby down a bit more and call Anna to say labour was starting. I knew she'd send a message out to our mom's group. As labour progressed, the thought of their prayers and emotional support encouraged me.

At supper, I mentioned casually to my mom and husband that Baby was on his way. I had a samosa and a bit of chicken and cauliflower, but I wasn't really hungry, especially since I knew labour would bring the food back up anyway. The girls liked the chicken, so it was a good thing I didn't need it to start labour, as we failed to make any of the East Indian food very spicy!

I kept moving through the evening, going to my room to do squats if a contraction was really hard. The older three girls got themselves ready for bed on their own and started a story on tape. Sunshine was excited to be sleeping in the recently rearranged blue room with her sisters, as it has the tape player. I helped Pearl into her jammies, turned on her white noise for her, and asked my mom to sit with her for a bit.

At 8:00 p.m., I paged my midwife to let her know that labour was going well. Contractions were four minutes apart. I got out my hot water bottle and sat in my rocking chair, praying and rocking through contractions.

When my husband got home, I told him the midwife was on her way and went to have a shower. She arrived, set up her things, and was ready to check on Baby and me when I got out of the shower. (Our condo, unfortunately, has a small hot water tank.)

After that, I laboured mostly in the bedroom. My second midwife arrived, and they chatted quietly about their equipment and what they needed. My husband got cold wash cloths for my face as labour began to make me hot. He refilled my juice and ginger ale for me and reheated the hot water bottle to put on my back or stomach. When I began throwing up, I took it as a good sign—labour was getting harder and would soon be over.

As my contractions continued, I got tired and impatient. I just wanted to be done and holding Baby. I asked my midwives about breaking my water and they agreed. I went for a shower again and began to feel like I had to push.

After a few more "pushy" contractions, I got out of the shower and returned to the bedroom. I had been excited for pushing to start, as it meant labour was almost done, but now it was just hard and painful. I reached down to feel Baby, thinking he should be nearly out, and he wasn't. I knelt by my bed and put my head down on my arms and wanted to cry.

My midwives remained patiently, quietly encouraging during this time. I stayed mostly at the side of the bed doing squats as I pushed because that's what felt good. For a while I had laboured in the bathroom, straddling the toilet or standing up to lean on the sink (and hoping it was installed well!). Now, I tried to stay where the midwives could see and help.

Finally, finally, Baby was getting close and the ring of fire began. My husband got more washcloths—cold ones for my face, hot ones for my bottom. When Baby's head came out, the midwives said something about his cord. One asked if I could get on the bed.

I hesitated, unsure what she meant—how was I going to move with Baby halfway out?—and then with another push, Baby was in my arms. His cord was tucked behind his arm and he howled his protests while the midwives worked to untangle it so we could lie down and snuggle.

They threw a warm towel over both of us, as I began to shiver. My mom, who'd gone to bed earlier, heard Baby's cries and came in to see him. The girls slept through all the noise (both mine and Baby's!). We rubbed down Baby as he continued to complain. My mom cut his cord.

Then she watched as the midwives weighed and checked him, and I went for my last shower.

Joey was almost nine pounds at birth, bigger than any of his sisters by a full pound. Maybe that's why pushing felt longer and harder than with any of them! Despite that, his was my shortest labour: around six hours compared to eight for Pearl and ten for the older three girls.

By midnight, Baby and I were tucked into bed with warm blankets around us. I was still cramping badly but otherwise tired and happy to be holding him. My mom went back to bed, and the midwives gathered their stuff and did their final checks of us.

It was lovely to have my mom to help for the next week. She woke up early with the girls and got them breakfast while I slept in. I napped every day with Joey while she took the girls to the park or swimming pool. She also cooked and cleaned so I could save the freezer meals I'd prepared for the week after she left. She was able to come to the girls' Christmas music recital and helped me get groceries for Joey's first outing.

CHAPTER FIFTY

Anna's Fifth and Sixth Births: Tangled Cords

After four girls, we proudly assumed we were a specialty shop. To our surprise, our fifth child was a little boy. He was born in the spring on Divine Mercy Sunday, which became rather poignant after we realized the danger he had been in.

My early labour was much like my previous few births. This time, right as he was crowning, the midwife calmly asked me to pause pushing. I did so with great effort while she carefully removed the cord that was wrapped around his neck.

"Slipping it off like a string of pearls," I remember her saying.

Our baby boy was born fine, and I didn't really realize how precarious things were until afterwards. The gentle yet professional manner of the midwives meant that the birth went smoothly despite the tanged cord.

At home, the girls were delighted with their little prince, with his tiny dark eyebrows over his huge, serious eyes. It was my first year homeschooling, and he was our biggest happy distraction for my kindergartener.

I do not wish to burden you with details of the story of our sixth birth, for it is a great source of sorrow. Our little girl Josephine didn't make it, as the cord was wrapped double about her neck and took her in early labour at home. She was thirty-eight weeks.

If you or a friend have suffered a stillbirth or miscarriage, you may find consolation in my poetry book, *unexpected blossoming: a journey of grief and hope,* which I published on Blurb to help other baby loss mamas feel less alone in their love and longing. To all others, may you never know such a loss!

CHAPTER FIFTY-ONE

Anna's Seventh Birth: Post-Loss

The reason I mentioned the stillbirth of my daughter is because this experience radically affected my subsequent pregnancies and births. I got pregnant only five months after losing my little Josephine and was in great emotional turmoil, as I found out on her six-month anniversary of loss.

This time, I felt stripped of the innocent illusion that a living baby was the guaranteed outcome of pregnancy. The world felt precarious and unsafe.

My midwives were amazingly supportive and very much accompanied me every step of the way. They allowed me to have an extra detailed ultrasound at thirty-three weeks, in order to check cord position. I wanted to go into labour knowing where things were at.

Thank goodness, the cord was nowhere near my baby boy's neck. I was relieved but still found it very hard to do any of the normal things, like buy newborn diapers. The one little wooden baby toy I bought for my son was an act of bravery for me.

My girlfriends were very caring and thoughtful, and rather than a celebratory baby shower, they held a blessing way for me, where the focus was on supporting the mother. My old friend Father McDonnell came and gave me a blessing for a safe labour, and we all prayed together. We had yummy food, and everyone spoiled me with caring gifts like flowers, bath salts, chocolates, cozy socks, etc.

Each friend took home a candle to light when they heard my labour was starting. It was so good not to feel alone with my fear; we were instead united in hope.

We decided to have our baby three weeks early, rather than my usual two, because it was felt that the thirty-eighth week would be too emotional for me.

On the day we chose for the birth, my midwife Carolyn came to my house first thing in the morning. She gave me a stretch and sweep and kept me company while I tried to drink the nasty labour cocktail. She made me laugh and even joined me in an '80s music living room dance party to help things along. She was there at every moment to check on the baby's heartbeat because my biggest fear was something going wrong before we got to the hospital.

She stepped out for lunch to give my husband and me time to go for spicy Indian food around the corner from our house. I started timing contractions as we ate. Carolyn met us back at our house. We went to the hospital together and had enough time to run the deep, hot birthing tub— my safe space to give birth.

My other midwife, Terry Lyn, came on shift early just to be there, and my OB came as well. I was so moved by their care and mentally knew I was safe. However, when I was fully dilated, my urge to push suddenly disappeared. I was paralyzed by the fear of the last-minute disaster.

"He is safe now; you can let him go," whispered my wise midwife, fully understanding my position.

With a big prayer and an act of faith, I summoned all my courage to push. My little one slipped safely into this world and into my eager arms.

I can't adequately express my joy and relief except to say that it still brings me to tears to think about it.

Being my seventh baby, and one born fairly soon after his older sister, I had terrible after-cramps and began to haemorrhage. I was hooked up to an oxytocin drip, and the next hour was the most painful of my life.

I was too stunned to properly advocate for myself and didn't request stronger pain medication than the standard Advil-Tylenol combo. It was not enough. My husband ordered us a pizza, as it was past the hospital dinner time, but I was in far too much pain to eat for some time, despite being ravenous.

Thank goodness with the next baby I requested strong pain meds for after the birth, and compared to the last time, they made me feel like I was lying on a Hawaiian beach, all happy and just fine.

I'm generally into natural medicine, but I couldn't be more grateful for those two little hydro-morphyn pills that made all the difference with baby birth number eight.

CHAPTER FIFTY-TWO

Anna's Eighth Birth

It seems to be some kind of mercy that often after a late loss, the next baby will be the opposite gender. This has happened to many of my baby-loss friends. Somehow, it makes things a little gentler, a little more different, and feels less like repeating history or "replacing" the child who passed away.

I felt more peaceful and ready when we found out we were having our next baby. My friend Kate dreamt I was pregnant with a baby girl before we even realized we were expecting. One day we went out for a mom sanity date (coffee, thrift shopping, and lunch) and decided to buy a pregnancy test for fun. I actually took the test in the bathroom of one of my favourite East Indian restaurants. As we soon discovered over our yummy roti rolls, Kate was right that I was pregnant!

I had just bought a pink coat, and we predicted she would be right about the gender as well. True! We were very happy to discover this at our twenty-week ultrasound, but it also hurt. Would this little girl make it? Even if she did, I would always miss my Josephine.

There were a lot of unhealed wounds in my heart, and I finally took the advice of my friend Rachel to get professional counselling. My therapist was a gentle, encouraging advocate who led me through various healing of memories activities. He helped me bring memories that were painful to the touch into the healing light of the present, where despite all difficulties, I was loved and safe and things were good. He helped me find my strength when I believed myself weak. He affirmed the best compliment I ever received as a mom from a woman on the bus as she looked at my six kids and told me, "You're a warrior!"

I believe it is primarily through this work that I was able to go through my next labour with courage and hope, without being paralyzed by fear. There was no stall in my labour this time. I highly recommend seeking professional help if you have lost a baby yourself. It is not a wound that heals alone. Also, seeking proper help for our struggles gives a good example of healthy self-care to our children and helps us be a more whole person to parent them.

On the day of the birth, I was in a rough place emotionally as both my mom and dad had recently entered the hospital, the first for heart issues, and the latter for a major cancer operation just before Christmas. My cholestasis was really bad; I believe stress aggravates this immune-related condition.

Rachel came over and took my kids to mom's group at our parish so I could have a quiet morning drinking my awful labour cocktail. I tried watching a funny movie to distract myself, but the castor oil smoothie did not stay down. I was exhausted. Rachel came back so I wouldn't be alone, while the other moms watched the kids.

I tried taking a nap, and in the mid-afternoon, Terry Lyn came to check on me and do a stretch and sweep. There was a pop and a rush of water, and this was our ticket to head straight to the hospital. Rachel slept over with her kids until my mother-in-law and sister-in-law could arrive to stay with my children.

Usually, my water only breaks when I start to push, so it was an unfamiliar experience to be dribbling water on the floor of the admitting room of the hospital. Getting admitted seemed to take forever, and we couldn't get a hold of the doctor replacing my OB, who was on holiday (I always have dual care, due to my cholestasis).

In the admitting room, Terry Lyn hooked up little TENS pads to my belly; when I felt a contraction, I pressed a button to release a little electronic pulse to ease the pain. It was a good distraction and helped a bit to have something to focus on.

Finally after dropping all our papers outside the elevator door and nearly losing my hat on the way, we were able to head upstairs.

Upstairs the halls seemed long and cold as I struggled with heavy contractions. It was around 4:30 p.m. When we got to the nurses' station, no one was there. I sat on the floor and jokingly threatened to have the baby right there. Terry Lyn looked at the nurse's clipboard and checked us into a room herself. I climbed on the bed with great relief and was nearly starting to push when the on-call doctor finally walked in the door.

For a moment they couldn't find the baby's heartbeat amidst the intense contractions. It was nearly 5:00 p.m., right around the time I think Josephine died. I caught my breath but fought despair.

"No! My job right now is only to push," I told myself. Shortly after, our baby girl slipped out like a selkie and beached herself on my chest. I kept feeling her little head and neck.

"No cord? No cord?" I asked.

"She's fine."

James and I both began to cry with relief. The nurses must have been confused so Terry Lyn gently explained.

After this it was all glory. As we had agreed, I had my strong pain meds, so the oxytocin drip needed to slow the bleeding didn't bother me. I asked James to warm up my favourite East Indian take-out that I had brought along, and had a hearty meal while he snuggled our baby girl.

This time I stayed in the hospital for three days, with my own cozy quilt, to rest and recover. It was a beautiful time to enjoy my new little one, read tons of my L.M. Montgomery novel *The Blythes Are Quoted*, and eat lots of good food, as the hospital finally allowed me to pick and order meals when I liked.

I hope by hearing these true stories of my babies' births, you can learn from my experiences, comforts, and mistakes, and become a great advocate for your baby and yourself a lot faster than I did.

More Resources

In a dozen years of growing and birthing babies, we've read a lot of books on pregnancy, childbirth, and newborns. Here are the books (and women!) who've influenced our birthing choices and ideas:

Rediscovering Birth by Sheila Kitzinger

Less a book on how to have a good birth and more a book on birth in general, this is an excellent resource. Sheila is a birth activist who looks at birthing practices around the world and through history.

I found this very helpful as it made me question some of our North American practices of birth (the common assumptions we make about how babies come) and be more open to trying something new (like squatting to deliver). I also appreciated the sense that Sheila gave of birth being a natural, womanly process, one I was uniquely equipped to perform.

Gentle Birth Choices by Barbara Harper

A registered nurse, Barbara talks about the options available to women in today's medical environment and what choices are the best for mom and baby. She questions the use of some technology (such as electronic fetal monitoring) during birth and shows how simpler can be better. Among the appendices in the back of her book, I found the birth plan I altered for Lily's birth. Like Sheila's book, Barbara's made me feel good about giving birth.

Ina May's Guide to Childbirth by Ina May Gaskin

In the first half of the book, Ina May tells a host of birth stories— stories radically different from those commonly shown on TV or in mainstream fiction.

In the second half of the book, she discusses things she learned as a midwife on a commune in Texas, helping women give birth at home without technology or drugs. Often funny (at some points I was laughing out loud and had to read paragraphs to my husband) and very factual, Ina May's book was a delight to read.

The Baby Book by **Dr. William Sears and Martha Sears**

William and Martha are the parents of eight children (including one adopted child); he's a doctor and she's a nurse. With their professional and personal experience, I trust them for good advice on parenting, birth, childhood illnesses, and more. *The Baby Book* is a bible of information about your child's first two years. Dr. Sears first introduced me to attachment parenting but also has tips for healthy pregnancy, good labour, and almost every question you'll face about raising your baby.

The Mindful Mom-to-Be by **Lori Bregman**

Written by an experienced birth doula, this book goes through pregnancy one month at a time, from the first month to labour and birth. Each chapter includes details about your changing body and your baby's growth, pregnancy exercises, journal ideas for mental and emotional preparation, and nutrition advice.

The chapters cover specific things to consider in each month of your pregnancy, from morning sickness in your second month to hemorrhoids in your eighth month. What I liked most about Bregman's book is all the very practical tips she includes.

In Praise of Stay-at-Home Moms by **Dr. Laura Schlessinger**

If you're planning to stay home with your kids, this book is a breath of fresh air. There is so much pressure in today's society to return to work after baby is born. As a SAHM, I've often felt looked down upon, as if my work in the home is not as important as my work outside the home could be.

With her no-nonsense style, Dr. Laura addresses the topic of SAHMs from the point of view of one who has been there, done that. She's also heard from many women, both working moms and stay-at-home moms. She talks about making the decision to be a stay-at-home mom and things that impact that decision. She also goes over a SAHM's "inner struggles"—this isn't an easy job.

Better Together: Because You're Not Meant to Mom Alone by Jill Savage and Anne McClane

Mother and daughter team Jill and Anne share what they've learned about mom friendships. Their book is full of practical advice for connecting with other moms—and why that's so important to us in today's world. Every chapter ends with Something to Think About and a Friendship Assignment. These are practical ways for you to apply what Jill and Anne have shared in making your own mom friends and building a supportive community of women around you.

unexpected blossoming: a journey of grief and hope by Anna Eastland.

unexpected blossoming chronicles the emotional journey of a bereaved mother the year after losing her daughter in labour. Intimate and passionate, these poems reflect the intensity of maternal love, the depths of grief, and the heart's amazing ability to heal.

When the usual words fail, this emotional companion serves as a gift to any mother grieving miscarriage or stillbirth, for there is strength in knowing one is not alone in suffering and surviving the loss of a child. Available online at www.blurb.ca/b/8204084-unexpected-blossoming.

Essential Oils: All-natural remedies and recipes for your mind, body and home.

This guide is an excellent introduction to using essential oils safely for a variety of purposes. They include a list of essential oils that are safe during pregnancy and recommendations for how to use oils during pregnancy or for babies.

About the Authors

Bonnie Way is a stay-at-home mom with five children ages 13 to 3. Each of her babies has been born in a different city with a different care provider. She has a B.A. in English (2006) and a B.A. in Writing (2014). She grew up in Alberta and now makes her home in Vancouver, BC. Bonnie is a homeschool graduate who is currently educating her oldest four children at home. She also blogs about motherhood, family travel, books and movies, and homeschooling as the Koala Mom (thekoalamom.com). She is the author of *North American Martyrs Kids Activity Book* and *Canadian Saints Kids Activity Book.*

Anna Eastland is a stay-at-home mom with nine children ages 14 to newborn (including one in heaven). Her babies have all been born in Vancouver with the same midwives. She grew up in Vancouver, the Sunshine Coast, and the Netherlands, and now lives in Vancouver, BC. She also homeschools her children and blogs about life as a mom at Just

East of Crazyland (eastofcrazyland.com). She's the author of *unexpected blossoming: a journey of grief and hope*, a book of poetry about stillbirth and baby loss. She is working on her second poetry book.

Bonnie and Anna both contributed to *Love Rebel: Reclaiming Motherhood*, along with three other mom bloggers. They actually wrote this anthology together before meeting in person! *Love Rebel* seeks to encourage and inspire moms in their journey.

You can find Bonnie on Instagram as @koalamomblog and on Facebook as @theKoalaBearWriter. Anna is @annaeastland on Twitter and @justeastofcrazy on Instagram. We love meeting fellow moms and chatting about all things birth, baby, and motherhood.

Love free printables?

Drop by the thekoalamom.com and subscribe to Bonnie's email newsletter to download six FREE printable resources, including

- Prayers for Pregnancy and Birth
- Party Planner
- Family Summer Bucket List

Manufactured by Amazon.ca
Acheson, AB

11076948R00103